For sharing my path and my passions,
thank you a thousand times,
grazie mille.

APPETITO

First edition printed in 2024 in the UK
ISBN: 978-1-915538-37-6

Written by: Alison Ranwell
www.alisonranwell.com

Edited by: Emily Readman & Phil Turner

Photography by: Alison Ranwell

Designed by: Paul Cocker

Sales: Emma Toogood

Contributors: Cara Snowden, Ben Doyle
& Sophia Derby

Printed by: Bell & Bain Ltd

Published by Meze Publishing Limited
Unit 1b, 2 Kelham Square
Kelham Riverside
Sheffield S3 8SD
Web: www.mezepublishing.co.uk
Telephone: 0114 275 7709
Email: info@mezepublishing.co.uk

APPETITO GLOSSARIO

Acqua di cottura - *'Cooking water', referring to the starchy water produced when cooking pasta. Often kept aside before straining the pasta in order to stir into sauces for a silky emulsion, it's an essential ingredient in Carbonara alla Romana (see page 85) and Paccheri allo Scarpariello (see page 69).*

Al dente - *When pasta is cooked so its inside remains a tiny bit harder and its shape and structure is maintained. Every box of pasta should have a precise al dente cooking time, but this can only truly be tested with a little bite using your teeth, i denti.*

Alveolatura - *The structure of the bubbles in baked bread which is formed by the type of yeast used as well as the folding technique and resting time. L'alveolatura can be 'open' with large holes or 'closed' with smaller, even bubbles.*

A pioggia - *'Like rain'. The method of pouring polenta gently into a pot of boiling water so it falls like rain.*

A tavola - *'At the table.' "How did you spend your Sunday?" – "A tavola". If the kitchen is the heart of the home, the table is the centre of this heart. It brings friends together for moments that go through the afternoon and into the night, and once you sit down at a table full of family and good food, it's hard to get up. A tavola is where the beautiful Italian culture of conversation, company and sharing happens, and where food, wine, coffee, crostata and digestivi simply become the bonds that tie us together.*

Buon appetito - *'Enjoy your meal'.*

Cucina povera - *'Poor cuisine'. An Italian style of cooking where every part of an ingredient is prized. The result is a less expensive but wholesome and delicious dish that relies on fragrant olive oil, kitchen garden produce, foraged foods and starches like pasta, polenta and stale bread. Orecchiette con Cime di Rapa (see page 91) is a perfect example of this style.*

Digestivo - *'Digestive'. A liqueur such as grappa, limoncello or Amaro Montenegro which is enjoyed at the end of a meal to 'aid digestion'.*

Ecco - *'Here you are!'*

È pronto - *'It's ready'. To welcome people to a meal that has just been placed on the table.*

Fare la scarpetta - *It is said the best part of Italian pasta is mopping up the sauce with some delicious bread, and you'll find some on every Italian table. Scarpetta means 'little shoe' but the precise origin of this phrase is vague. Some claim it refers to the shoe shape of the bread, others say it's like the bottom of a shoe picking up whatever it finds on the street!*

La mantecatura - *The process of stirring butter, cheese, or both into a risotto (or Scarpariello on page 69) during the last few minutes of cooking to create a creamy texture.*

Mountain food - *A term we use in this book quite a bit. In recipes like Canerderli (see page 123) or Polenta e Gorgonzola (see page 161), you'll notice this expression is used to describe a style of cooking found in regions of higher altitudes. We've come to anticipate and cherish this hearty kind of cuisine that's unique to the 'mountains'.*

Passaverdura - *A manual food mill that mashes vegetables but keeps the skins and pips separate. Perfect for the end of summer when bottling tomato sauce.*

Pinzimonio - *A simple mix of vinegar and extra-virgin olive oil used as a dip for bread or placed on a tagliere (see page 17) to dunk vegetables into.*

Primo - *Meaning the 'first' course; and* **secondo**, *'second'. In Italy, you're generally expected to have both, plus the* **antipasto** *(starter),* **contorni** *(sides) and* **dolce** *(dessert) – and coffee if you're taking lunch seriously. But there's no need to rush - the time to eat, talk, and savour your meal is the key ingredient in Italian cuisine, meaning you can easily get through a four or five course meal nessun problema - no problem. All you need is a long, lazy Sunday afternoon and some good company.*

Pugnetto - *'A little fist'. Used to describe how much coarse salt to add to the pasta pot. A little handful is about 2 tablespoons.*

Ragù - *Essentially a thick pasta sauce beginning with un soffritto. Traditionally, meat is used (beef, veal, pork, rabbit or donkey), but ragù di lenticchie (lentil ragù) also exists as a vegetarian option.*

(Un) Soffritto - *Italy's classic combination of equal parts diced onion, celery and carrot which are fried gently and used as a base for soups, meat sauces, and stews.*

Sugo - *Simply: 'sauce'.*

CONTENTS

ANTIPASTI

PRIMI PASTA

PRIMI ALTRI

SECONDI

CONTORNI

DOLCI

INTRODUZIONE

The decision to move countries is exciting but equally scary. I'd been longing for empty, green spaces, so when a last-minute teaching job came up in Veneto, I left London in a heartbeat with just a small suitcase and maybe five Italian words to my name. There's a lot to be said for uprooting oneself – I discovered I was a foodie.

They'd said the small city of Conegliano was beautiful, with its hilltop castle positioned perfectly between the sea and the mountains; between the Adriatic and the Dolomites. They'd forgotten to mention the rolling prosecco hills that turned gold in autumn or the warmth of strangers who welcomed me with friendship. We'd sit in chestnut groves at long, chequered tables for lazy lunches that went into the night or visit breathtaking ancient cities and pointy Dolomite peaks that shone pink at dusk. Splintered doors would open into bustling *osterie* and village squares would pack out in *sagra* festivities in the picturesque haze that was my first year in Italy.

I rented a tiny house with an oversized fireplace at my friend Graziella's *agriturismo*, where twice a year for two weeks I'd have to leave so they could hang freshly made *sopressa* from the downstairs wooden beams, the fat dripping as the *sopressa* cured in the heat and smoke of a slight fire. Having grown up in South Africa, where construction might be a couple of hundred years old, it was extraordinary to step onto the 2000-year-old stone path that led through the mountains to Bavaria and passed just behind the *agriturismo*. I'd stare in awe of the rusty plaque beside the Roman road stating 'Via Claudia Augusta, 47 AD' before treading where thousands had walked before.

A year or so later, after picking up enough spoken Italian, partly thanks to Graziella's seven-year-old nephew, Italy's true nature began to emerge. I found *la dolce vita* was not one of frivolous spritz-sipping on a Venetian piazza but a deeper rooted 'sweet life' in the layers of this passionate country; a place where authenticity and origin are valued in most things, including food.

The first memory I have of 'producing' food was in my early teens when I bought a pasta machine. I took up making fresh spaghetti on Saturday afternoons in Cape Town, cooking *amatriciana* by the batch to sell to my mom's teacher friends. I can't remember if I sold much – it's a vague recollection and I think they simply humored an entrepreneurial 13-year-old – because the memory of making Italian food that shines the brightest is from Barnes near London. Still in my teens, in a galley kitchen one-person-wide, my uncle and I set out to make *pesto alla genovese* one lunchtime, the Italian way. He's an old-school foodie, so we sat on two wooden chairs facing each other; I held the stone mortar and ground the pesto while he drizzled the olive oil. It was a lengthy process with not much to show for it, but what a worthy result it was. The reminiscent perfume of crushed basil leaves and the effort it took is as clear to me now as it was all those years ago.

There's an immense amount of love in Italian food, and I believe this is the key ingredient that makes it stand out from the rest: a love of good food, love for those at your table, and a love for your territory and its produce. In Italy, food is never just food. Nowadays in particular, it's so important to know what we eat and where it comes from. I found this communal passion in Italy.

Intent on bringing Francesco's mum's lasagne to the Midlands, it was this culture of 'food as love' that I was inspired to share when we swapped our seemingly idyllic life of Italian hamlets and forests full of *funghi* for the cathedral city of Lichfield in England.

Cooking family favourites from home, I started Mangia Mangia during a time when so much was lost but a true appreciation of genuine food was found: the Covid pandemic. After building our small business by attending local markets and pushing flyers through letterboxes on Saturday mornings, my mother-in-law's beloved Sunday dish, with its signature 'Nonna Lili Layer', became our business' main feature. Encouraging the traditional Italian culture of celebrating seasonal and honouring local, we sourced farm produce as part of Lichfield's vibrant food scene and adapted our dishes to the seasons. One year later, we gleefully perfected Francesco's risotto to an authentic cook-at-home version and introduced the art of l'aperitivo with our pop-up spritz bar, Aperitivo Time. I say "we" as Mangia Mangia has always been a family project with our girls in the kitchen, on the market stall, and mixing spritzes at summer festivals.

"Mangia mangia!" – "Eat up, eat up!" – is something you hear all the time in Italy, especially at Nonna Lili's kitchen table. With our customers looking forward to chocolate salami at Christmas, or excitedly ordering their faves through our website for weekend delivery, I've found that owning a small business is long hours and hard work but also indescribably rewarding. My favourite part about having a stall in the Producers' Market is delighting in the communal joy of uniting in discussions about food, and I believe the best way to enjoy food is to share it. So, here's an intimate collection of our family's favourites, our go-to meals guided by the seasons, recipes handed down through generations, and the dishes we seek out on our travels.

Besides bringing inspiring Italian to your table, this book delves into the soul of Italian cuisine, transporting you to 'Life in Italy', where good food seems to be the subtext to every beautiful conversation. As our family collection, Appetito wouldn't be complete without a hefty helping of pasta dishes and recipes in quirky places, like having gorgonzola and polenta as a main, or *pesto alla genovese* as an *antipasto*; there are pasta types in the plural, Italian food expressions which may surprise you, and culinary legends carved in stone; there's also a lot of tiramisù because we've included your favourites, too.

Buon appetito and happy cooking!
Alison

ANTiPASTi

Mercato Centrale, Firenze

BRUSCHETTA TOSCANA
TUSCAN BRUSCHETTA

The first recipe in our cookbook is also the simplest one. There are six ingredients in a classic Tuscan bruschetta; *in effetti*, it's just bread and tomatoes, but it stands as one of the most iconic Italian foods of all time. It certainly is for me.

Taste has no relation whatsoever to price in Tuscany, where the food makes you stop in your tracks. From *finocchiona* to *fiorentina*, it's this region that left me with the most memorable food experiences from the most basic of ingredients.

When I think of Tuscany, I think of golden wheat fields and warm, yellow sun; dirt tracks, shrill cicada song, ancient ruins and Volterra. It was another blue-sky day when I parked *la macchina rossa* (the red car) outside the hilltop city walls and walked through one of Volterra's Etruscan gates. On a solo Tuscan adventure with barely any Italian proficiency or lire to my name, the first thing that happened was lunch. And here was the stop-in-your-tracks moment.

Lunch was bruschetta and a glass of local red wine at a wobbly *trattoria* table for one on a worn stone road. A garlic clove rubbed onto toasted Tuscan bread and topped with chopped tomatoes and a drizzle of olive oil - the stuff of the gods. There are very few meals that burn a memory into your brain; I'm sure you can think of one, too. But how does the simplest combination of garlic, unsalted bread, and tomatoes achieve this?

In those days, we used camera film and the *'vecchia lira'*, a currency as nonsensical to me as the paperwork required to accomplish anything official. Italian offices loved a *timbro* (rubber stamp) and a signature on every page of every document, especially back then before the world went digital. One-thousand lire was equal to a mere 50c, so there were multitudes of zeros. Having moved to Italy only six months before embarking on a road trip, my Italian was incredibly patchy. Italian is a gesticular language, meaning they use their hands to talk; for this reason, I could get by with pointing for a very long time, although phone conversations always proved a challenge. There's something to be said for Italians in general: they're a warm, loving population who adore the spoken voice. To hear a foreigner attempt their beautiful language brings only happiness. They had all the time in the world to listen to an English lady ask for "space for one" on the phone, just as I had all the time to drive from campsite to campsite and enquire in person with a point and a nod if the phone signal was bad.

On a strict budget of 90,000 lire per day (about 45 euros), I had 20 euros for accommodation, 15 euros for food and 10 for petrol - if I stayed in campsites I could save quite a bit. My days were spent perusing the road map and deciding where to visit, or randomly taking side roads I loved the look of. I'd drive up to hilltop towns like Montalcino, park outside the city walls and go inside to explore. I'd blow the budget on red wine and plates of pasta, sit in sunny piazzas and smile at how grand life was. I'd pick a cheap hotel from the Lonely Planet guide, call them, and ask for a room in broken Italian, or turn down a street at a 'CAMPING' sign, ready to pitch my tent with a stash of Pecorino, Chianti, and a good book.

Simple foods in Italy are sublime because every ingredient is divine. In Tuscany, 20-odd years ago, one could easily get by on 30,000 lire and eat like a king. While this humble bruschetta may not look much like royalty, if you seek out the ripest tomatoes and loveliest bread, just add a drizzle of good olive oil and you've got yourself a feast.

BRUSCHETTA TOSCANA
TUSCAN BRUSCHETTA

PREPARATION TIME: 20 MINUTES WITH 30 MINUTES STANDING TIME | SERVES 6

INGREDIENTS

500g ripe Italian tomatoes

Pinch of sea salt

Extra-virgin olive oil

12 basil leaves

1 clove of garlic

6 thick slices of ciabatta, sourdough or crusty bread

PREPARATION

1. Begin by washing the tomatoes and slicing them up into small chunks; the smaller, the better.

2. Add a pinch of salt and a drizzle of olive oil and half of the basil leaves ripped into pieces and mix together in a bowl.

3. Cover and let stand for at least 30 minutes.

4. Peel a clove of garlic and slice in half, lengthways.

5. When ready to serve, toast the bread under a grill or in a pan, keeping an eye on how brown it becomes, and flip the slices over to toast both sides.

6. Rip the remaining basil leaves and add to the tomatoes whilst the bread is toasting.

7. When toasted, rub the sliced clove of garlic onto one side of the warm bread and spoon the tomatoes on top with their juice.

8. Drizzle a little olive oil onto each bruschetta before tucking in.

COOK'S NOTES

Bruschetta makes an excellent antipasto you can prepare in advance. The tomatoes can be made up to 3 hours before and kept in a cool corner of the kitchen, although they are best at room temperature so if you do need to refrigerate, then remove them an hour before assembling.

Any tomatoes can be used, large or small, but ensure they are deep red and ripe.

Turn your Tuscan Bruschetta into a main course by placing a mozzarella di bufala or burrata on top with a couple of anchovy fillets, sun-dried tomatoes, capers or olives, and don't forget that glass of Tuscan red.

Abbazia di Galgano, Siena

re di Pisa, Toscana

Valdorcia, Toscana

UN TAGLIERE
MEAT AND CHEESE BOARD

Every region in Italy celebrates their unique blend of foods, traditions and dialects. This goes for the heights of the Dolomite peaks and lush valleys of northern Alto Adige to the dusty olive groves in southern Sicily and everything in between.

We love sampling local dishes on our travels and uncovering a wealth of diversity in regional foods. The perfect shortcut to an area's specialities, and our favourite thing to order wherever we end up, is *un tagliere*.

Tagliere stems from the word '*tagliare*' - to cut. That's just what this is: a chopping board of sliced meats and cheeses.

Ordering *un tagliere* is always a little bit of a gamble, but we've found you can never go wrong. Good food is embedded in national pride, and the love that goes into local produce turns it into a celebration every time.

The beauty of a meat and cheese board is often the variety of what's on it. In Tuscany, a love of sweet and savoury sees chestnut honey or pickled vegetables in vinegar (*la giardiniera*) paired with sharp Pecorino cheese. In the foodie capital of Emilia Romagna, you can expect *mortadella*, Bologna's gigantic polony, known fondly as '*la bologna*', and *prosciutto di Parma*. Here too, you may find sweet sauces or fruit compotes, fresh figs, or a slice of melon and, of course, you'll be offered a bright red glass of sparkling Lambrusco.

It seems silly to write a recipe for *un tagliere*. After all, a meat and cheese board is sometimes simply a collection of what you have in your kitchen, or whatever you might find in your local cheese shop. We've given you guidelines based on our Mangia Mangia *antipasti* platters as inspiration for your own.

To create an Italian *tagliere*, find the cured meats section in your deli or supermarket and go wild! The other beauty of *un tagliere* is discovering something new. Slice up some fruit and fresh bread or raid your cracker cupboard. Why not try pairing cheeses with preserves or sweet pickles you may have hiding at the back of your fridge?

Place your board on the table and dive in. One of the best ways to enjoy food is to share it.

UN TAGLIERE
MEAT AND CHEESE BOARD

PREPARATION TIME: 15 MINUTES | SERVES 6

INGREDIENTS

FRUITS AND VEGETABLES
1 pear or apple

½ lemon, freshly squeezed

150g black or green grapes, figs and/or apricots

100g baby Italian tomatoes

CONDIMENTS
Extra-virgin olive oil

Modena balsamic vinegar

50g Pesto alla genovese (see page 25) and/or olive tapenade

6 tbsp fruit compote or honey

CURED MEATS
100g salame, coppa or sopressa

150g bresaola or mortadella

150g prosciutto crudo (Parma ham)

CHEESES
150g gorgonzola or blue cheese

150g Parmigiano Reggiano, Grana Padano or Pecorino Romano

100g soft goat's cheese, stracchino or robiola

ANTIPASTI
100g stuffed peppers and/ or pickled garlic

80g green or black olives

100g caper berries, sun-dried tomatoes and/ or pickled artichokes

1 ciabatta, Italian breadsticks, taralli or a tray of Focaccia Pugliese (see page 197)

TO SERVE
30x40 cm wooden board or tray, plus small dipping pots

PREPARATION

1. Begin by washing, coring and slicing the fruit. Use a squeeze of fresh lemon to 'wash' the apple and pear slices to prevent discolouration.

2. Make some pinzimonio by mixing olive oil and balsamic vinegar. Put the pesto and tapenade into small dipping pots and drizzle the tops with olive oil to prevent them drying out.

3. Remove the rind and slice up the gorgonzola. Slice the salame and mortadella, too, if using.

4. Chop the aged cheeses (Parmigiano, etc.) into 1cm chunks and begin to place the fruits and vegetables onto the board along with the pots of dipping sauces.

5. Add the olives, pickles, the meat and then the cheese.

6. Place the bread and breadsticks into a separate basket or scatter directly onto the table.

7. Serve immediately.

COOK'S NOTES

You can prepare un tagliere 2 hours in advance and cover the entire board with cling film to keep in the fridge. The flavours are best at room temperature, so remove 20 minutes before placing on the table.

Even if certain pairings are a classic in Italy, like gorgonzola and pear, feel free to mix and match a range of meats, cheeses, dips, fruits, vegetables, pickles and delicious goodies.

PESTO DI LIMONI
LEMON PESTO

The region of Campania in southern Italy basks in glorious sunshine, and we all love to lap it up on the Sorrento Coast which produces some of the biggest, tastiest fruit in Italy. San Marzano tomatoes, which are used in traditional Neapolitana pizza sauce, come exclusively from a tiny piece of land just south of Mount Vesuvius. While we all know that Sorrento lemons make the best limoncello, did you know they also make a *favoloso* pesto?

Lemons, almonds, Pecorino Romano and garlic crushed in a mortar is one of the best things you can put on pasta. Pesto is often just a mix of what you have around, but there's an 'official' pesto recipe featuring Campania lemons that brings with it a zingy flavour and a nostalgic sea breeze from Procida, a small island in the Gulf of Naples.

Procida's colourful cluster of pastel homes welcomes fishing boats into its picture-book village harbour, and you may recognise it as the setting for the film *The Talented Mr Ripley*. Postcard-perfect, it's the quaintest of islands and is also home to the largest of lemons.

The lemons of Procida have such thick, delicious pith that you can eat the entire fruit, and locals call them '*pan di Procida*' or 'bread of Procida'. Amongst other things, they're pounded into a pesto to stir through freshly cooked spaghetti in one of southern Italy's most classic of pasta dishes, *spaghetti al pesto di limoni di Procida*.

We love this pesto with any kind of pasta but find it works especially well with *tortiglioni* because the ridges hold the sauce just perfectly. As an *antipasto*, *pesto di limoni* makes a beautiful summery dipping sauce for *un tagliere* (see page 21) and is delicious on bruschetta with chunks of buffalo mozzarella and ripped basil leaves.

You can, of course, use any lemons, but make sure they are unwaxed and as natural as possible.

PESTO DI LIMONI
LEMON PESTO

PREPARATION TIME: 20 MINUTES | SERVES 4

INGREDIENTS

50g pine nuts or almonds

1 clove of garlic (optional)

1 bunch of flat-leaf parsley, washed

1 Procida lemon, juiced and zested (or two unwaxed lemons, but do not use the pith)

80g Parmigiano Reggiano, grated

Drizzle of extra-virgin olive oil

PREPARATION

1. Using a pestle and mortar, pound the nuts into a paste with the garlic, if you are using it (see the notes for how to use a handheld blender).

2. Add the washed parsley leaves, the juice and zest of the lemons (use the pith of Procida lemons, if using) and then begin to sprinkle in the Parmigiano and drizzle in the olive oil, pounding until you achieve a smooth consistency.

COOK'S NOTES

Pesto can be stored in a jar in the fridge. Simply drizzle some olive oil on top to discourage oxidisation (where the pesto turns brown) and use within 4 days of making. You can also freeze it for up to a month without the cheese, which you can add once it's defrosted.

Another option is to use a handheld immersion blender to mix all the ingredients together at once. Add more lemon juice and olive oil if the pesto is too thick to blend.

Before adding pesto to pasta or gnocchi, stir in a ladle of hot cooking water to melt it into a delicious, silky sauce while your pasta or gnocchi is on the boil.

Casa della Venere in Conchiglia, Pompeii

PESTO ALLA GENOVESE
BASIL PESTO FROM GENOVA

Pestare is a widely used word in Italian, not only for food. It can mean 'press' as in *pestare l'uva* (press grapes), 'step on' as in *pestare i fiori* (step on flowers), or 'pound' as in *pestare l'acqua nel mortaio* (pound water in a mortar, used figuratively when talking about something that has no use).

From *pestare* comes pesto, the pounded product. In Italy, the word has many versions and pesto does too, with the most well-known being *pesto alla genovese*, pesto from Genova.

The foodie legend of pesto is more historical than fairy-tale, and it originates in ancient Rome with a paste called *moretum*, which was made of crushed garlic, cheese and herbs. At the time, the people of Genova had their own version named *agliata* which was made from garlic and walnuts, much like *pesto alla genovese*. When merchant ships travelled between ports, produce would change hands and recipes would adapt to include whatever local ingredients were available. An example of this is the rosy-pink, Sicilian *pesto alla trapanese*, made with tomatoes, almonds and basil. As the herb was prized by the Romans for its alleged healing powers, basil soon became known and grown in Liguria, too.

Italy's trick to culinary excellence lies in simple but beautiful ingredients - gorgeous *salame* on gorgeous bread always makes a gorgeous *panino*. Seeing as pesto is also made from hardly any ingredients, ensure these are top quality and, if possible, DOP (*Denominazione d'Origine Protetta*) - a.k.a PDO (Protected Designation of Origin). Grown in specified areas of Italy and having passed rigorous quality checks, these regional specialities will make your dish sing.

You'll notice the use of a wooden pestle in traditional methods: this is to ensure no flavours are altered during preparation, as the joy is in how the genuine ingredients come together quickly to be eaten straight away. Marble is the mortar of choice but only because it traditionally always has been.

A specific type of basil from Liguria with tiny, fragrant leaves must be used for official *pesto alla genovese*, but any fresh basil works well for this beautiful, flavourful condiment that you can enjoy in so many ways. We love to buy potted kitchen basil in England; it's readily available year-round and grown in Britain. There's something so satisfying about cutting the leaves from the plant to go straight into your food, and nutrient-wise there's nothing more vibrant.

Pesto alla genovese is Liguria's pride and joy, along with the stunning UNESCO coastal park of the Cinque Terre. So, yes, they are smugly picky about basil and, of course, the olive oil must be Riviera Ligure DOP and their chosen pasta must be hand-rolled *trofie* (a short, thin, twisted pasta). Something you don't see much outside of Italy is the Ligurian preference for pesto with green beans. Steamed, chopped and added to pasta or gnocchi, you'll find this dish on most Cinque Terre menus and on page 25 of this recipe book. If you can source a crisp white wine or a cold bottle of Pigato from the terraced vineyards of Liguria, then pair it with this classic recipe for an authentic treat that's sure to conjure up the pastel villages and rocky bays of Italy's beautiful Cinque Terre region.

Buon appetito!

PESTO ALLA GENOVESE
BASIL PESTO FROM GENOVA

PREPARATION TIME: 20 MINUTES | SERVES 4-6

INGREDIENTS

50g Parmigiano Reggiano (preferably aged 36 months)

10g Pecorino Romano (preferably aged 15 months)

80g basil leaves

2 cloves of garlic

Sea salt, to taste

2 tbsp pine nuts

80ml extra-virgin olive oil

PREPARATION

1. Grate the cheese and wash and dry the basil leaves, being careful not to crush or bruise them.
2. Peel the garlic and, using a pestle, pound in a mortar with a pinch of sea salt until smooth.
3. Add the pine nuts and basil leaves with a drizzle of oil and keep pounding, stopping every so often to add more oil.
4. When the pesto is a smooth and uniform paste, gently mix in the cheese.
5. Test for salt and adjust accordingly.

COOK'S NOTES

Pesto can be stored in a jar in the fridge. Simply drizzle some olive oil on top to discourage oxidisation (where the pesto turns brown) and use within 4 days of making. You can also freeze it for up to a month without the cheese, then stir it into the defrosted pesto or add it directly onto your dish if serving pasta or gnocchi.

Mix the pesto with l'acqua di cottura (pasta cooking water) to melt it into a delicious, silky sauce while your pasta or gnocchi is on the boil.

Any hard, aged Italian cheese will work well if you can't find Pecorino or Parmigiano. For example, we often use Grana Padano, aged for 18 months.

Not everyone has time to sit and pound away at a marble mortar, and not everyone has a mortar. The best thing about pesto is the consistency and flavour obtained by crushing an ingredient instead of chopping it. Crushing basil stops it from changing colour, and crushing garlic increases the flavours tenfold, but using a food processor is ten times quicker (and easier). Honestly, this recipe will still taste incredible whichever way you make it.

Another good option is a handheld blender. If you have enough liquid and/or olive oil, the sauce has no time to discolour. I find making pesto alla genovese is a doddle with my immersion blender; add a squeeze of fresh lemon juice to ensure a vibrant, green sauce while working as quickly as possible.

Le Cinque Terre, Liguria

Tellaro, Liguria

INSALATA DI POLPO
OCTOPUS SALAD

We've always called this dish *Insalata di Polpo*, or Octopus Salad, but Nonna Lili says around Venice, octopus is known as *piovra*. *Polpo, piovra* and *moscardini* are all considered 'octopus' and adored in Italian cooking.

You'll find this delicious salad served warm or cold with olives, capers and pickled peppers, or with tomatoes, potatoes and celery. There are so many versions throughout Italy which vary according to what grows locally.

Most towns have a weekly market day, usually with a fish counter. One of the most impressive is Venice's Rialto Fish Market where Venetians select their seafood from 7.30 a.m. in the beautiful neo-gothic Loggia Maggiore della Pescheria, built in 1907 to host covered markets beside the Gran Canal.

A market is fantastic for many reasons, but mainly because it's a collection of local foods, customs, and quirky traits that make every town unique. It's a welcoming space where children, pets, and people of all ages are drawn out onto the streets, sometimes in the worst of weather, and where one can stock up on fruits, vegetables, bread and cheese. It's always astounding how quickly and neatly everything suddenly manages to disappear at closing time. After lunch, the city streets return to how they were and traffic flows through town again. If you think about it, the weekly market has been around forever; perhaps that's why it's so efficient.

Friday is a special day in Italy known as *Venerdi Pesce* – Fish (or Seafood) Friday. It holds a special place in religious tradition as a day of restraint, and over the years it has developed into a day where fish is on the menu and on the table, instead of meat. If your town's market happens to fall on a Friday, expect long queues at the fish counter, a mass of early shoppers, and an abundance of beautiful seafood your jaw will simply drop at. It's here you'll find your octopus.

INSALATA DI POLPO
OCTOPUS SALAD

PREPARATION TIME: 30 MINUTES, PLUS 1 HOUR COOLING TIME | COOKING TIME: 30 MINUTES | SERVES 6-8

INGREDIENTS

1 large octopus (approximately 1kg)

2 large potatoes

300g baby Italian tomatoes, halved

50g taggiasca olives, pitted

20g flat-leaf parsley, washed and chopped

Drizzle of extra-virgin olive oil

½ lemon, juiced

Salt and pepper, to taste

COOK'S NOTES

Octopus salad can be kept covered in the fridge for 3 days and served cold, but its flavours are always best at room temperature. The taggiasca olives can be substituted for any small Mediterranean olives.

Celery is lovely in this salad for added crunch, and some families add pickled artichokes, peppers or capers.

If you can't find flat-leaf parsley, you can use curly, although the flavour will be less intense.

PREPARATION

1. Remove the octopus' ink sac by delicately squeezing it out, then remove the eyes and any insides from the octopus' head. (Fishmongers will do this if you ask them to, and it's often already prepared this way when you buy it.) Wash the whole octopus in cold water.

2. Bring a deep pot of water to the boil and dip the tentacles in and out of the water until they curl. Then, place the entire octopus underwater so that it is covered. Simmer for 20 minutes, then poke a toothpick through the thickest part to test if the flesh is tender. Simmer for longer, if required (this depends on the size of the octopus, so test at 10-minute intervals).

3. Meanwhile, peel and boil the potatoes in a separate pot of salted water until cooked, then cool under cold running water and chop them into 1.5cm pieces.

4. When the octopus is tender, turn off the heat but leave the octopus to cool in the water - this keeps the flesh soft.

5. After an hour, the octopus should be cold enough to handle. Using your fingers, remove the 'slime' between the tentacles and chop the octopus into 1.5cm chunks, making sure to discard the beak and inner cartilage.

6. Add the cooked potatoes, tomatoes, olives, chopped parsley, and a generous dressing of olive oil, lemon juice, salt and pepper to a bowl with the octopus. Toss to combine and serve lukewarm or at room temperature.

Orate in Gargano
€ al kg 20,00

Piovre   Pescate
Octopus vulgaris   Polpi veraci
Pescate in Oceano Atlantico est Fao 34,
con reti da traino - scongelato
consumare previa cottura
Al kg 20,00

Mercato di Pesce, Treviso, Veneto

Mercato della Pignasecca, Napoli

Canal Grande, Trieste

CAPESANTE GRATINATE
BAKED SCALLOPS

The grand city and seaport of Trieste dominates Italy's coastline at a prominent northern position on the Adriatic Sea, and Piazza Unità d'Italia, known as Europe's largest seaside square, opens before her cruise ship visitors. Lined with resplendent neo-classical *palazzi* and busy cafes, the underrated Italian art of *il dolce far niente* (sweet idleness) is easily achieved here.

In Trieste, the so-called City of Coffee and home to iconic brand Illy, you're enticed by piazzas and wide streets stacked with endless amounts of chairs and tables, each ready to welcome you to sit and sip a coffee, take in the views, enjoy an aperitivo and simply do nothing - *fare niente*.

Due to autonomous status, the Friuli region isn't subdivided into provinces and can celebrate its uniquely diverse character. Here, a melting pot of Slovenian, Croatian, Austrian, German, and Italian cultures come together with ease, resulting in an enchanting mix of architecture, language and especially cuisine.

Seafood is freshly fished from the Adriatic and needs little condiment for its flavours to be truly appreciated. Indeed, Trieste's simple baked scallop recipe has spread to all corners of the country as a prized *antipasto*, and we're often greeted by it at special celebrations around Nonna Lili's kitchen table.

Scallops are usually sold pre-cleaned in their frilly, fan shells at a fishmongers or fish counter. They make the perfect introduction to a seafood meal, but if you can't find the shells, simply bake the scallops in an ovenproof dish and serve them on pretty little plates for equal flair.

CAPESANTE GRATINATE
BAKED SCALLOPS

PREPARATION TIME: 5 MINUTES | COOKING TIME: 15 MINUTES | SERVES 2-4

INGREDIENTS

2 tbsp flat-leaf parsley, chopped

16g breadcrumbs

Salt and pepper, to taste

4 scallops, in their shells

4 splashes dry white wine, vermouth or brandy

4 generous knobs of butter

PREPARATION

1. Preheat the oven to 180°c (160°c fan/gas mark 4) and begin by combining the parsley and breadcrumbs in a bowl, then season with salt and pepper to taste.

2. Clean the scallops by loosening them from their shells, cutting away the light brown part but keeping the orange coral and white mussel. Give the shells and scallops a good wash and pat them dry with some kitchen towel.

3. Put the scallops back in their shells and cover each one with a quarter of the crumb mix, a splash of wine, vermouth or brandy and a generous knob of butter.

4. Bake for 10 to 15 minutes and, when golden, put one or two on each plate as a delicious starter.

COOK'S NOTES

If you can't find the shells, lightly oil an ovenproof dish and bake using the same ingredients. Put two scallops onto each plate and pour the buttery sauce over them to serve.

BRESAOLA, RUCOLA E GRANA
BRESAOLA, ROCKET AND GRANA SALAD

The history of *bresaola* is an ancient one. *Alla fine*, it's salted and aged meat - in this case beef - but salting meat as a preservation method has existed for eons. Some say the word *bresaola* originates from the name of an early curing process where coals, called *brasa*, were used to keep the environment dry while the meat was delicately flavoured with bay leaves and juniper berries that were placed directly onto the embers. No one can be certain, however, as the pronunciation is only loosely connected. The second syllable, '*sa*', on the other hand, can easily be linked to the word '*sale*' - salt.

Traces of similarly salted meats have historically been found in the Swiss Alps and, indeed, *bresaola* is very much a 'mountain food', known in Italy as a speciality from Valtellina near the Swiss-Italian border. The climatic conditions, especially the Alpine winds which help to dry the meat, are particular to this region.

This cured meat remained 'native' to the area until the early 1800s when it began to be produced industrially and its popularity reached further afield, becoming well-known throughout the rest of Italy and eventually abroad. Versions of cured lean beef were made in a similar fashion from different cuts of meat until the Valtellina locals asked for their product to be geographically protected to maintain its authenticity. *Bresaola di Valtellina* successfully received IGP status in 1992, meaning that any other salted beef outside of the territory must be called by another name.

The meat is dark red, almost purple, and shaped like a *salame*, so you'd immediately spot it amongst the *prosciutti* at the *banco della gastronomia* (the deli counter). Whenever we choose *bresaola* from the cold meat counter, we're always asked: 'Beef or horse?' While the Valtellina product is strictly beef according to IGP guidelines, *bresaola* is commonly made from both in north Italy's Piemonte and Veneto regions where, in the provinces of Asti and Padova in particular, horse meat is very popular.

Looking almost identical, *bresaola di cavallo* (horse) is slightly darker in colour, but the taste is like the beef version, with only a marginal variation in the intensity of its flavour. Either can be used in this much-loved Italian combo; you'll find *bresaola*, rocket and Grana Padano as an *antipasto*, in *tramezzini* (an Italian sandwich), on bruschetta and on pizza.

BRESAOLA, RUCOLA E GRANA
BRESAOLA, ROCKET AND GRANA SALAD

PREPARATION TIME: 10 MINUTES | SERVES 4

INGREDIENTS

60g rocket, washed

Sea salt, to taste

Drizzle of extra-virgin olive oil

150g bresaola, thinly sliced

50g Grana Padano

Modena balsamic vinegar

PREPARATION

1. Dress the rocket with a pinch of sea salt and a drizzle of olive oil.

2. Arrange the rocket on a plate or board and carefully place each slice of bresaola on top.

3. Shave the Grana Padano onto the bresaola using a knife, being extra careful to cut away from yourself.

4. Drizzle the salad with balsamic vinegar and serve immediately.

COOK'S NOTES

Lemon juice is often recommended in recipes with bresaola, but it isn't used much or advised in Italy as it oxidises the meat almost immediately.

This salad calls for Modena balsamic vinegar as it's one of bresaola's besties and a beautiful condiment. Find a lovely, aged one for a deeper flavour. You can also try balsamic glaze.

Bresaola changes colour quickly, so to keep its vibrant hue, serve this salad straight away.

Montaner, Veneto

INSALATA CAPRESE
CAPRESE SALAD

Served all over Italy in *trattorie* (restaurants), and on lunch tables as a starter, this iconic *antipasto* screams *"Italia!"* - not only because of the red, green and white colours of her flag (*il tricolore*), but also for its most quintessential of Italian ingredients.

Sometime between World Wars, the Caprese Salad was born. This is not to say that mozzarella, tomato and basil have never come together on a plate, but they were never given an official name until sometime in the mid-20th century.

The dilemma still remains, however, of who gets to claim the fame.

Undoubtedly, this salad is from the famous isle of Capri, and is potentially equally as famous, but who knew that the founder of futurism, Marinetti, a local builder, and the King of Egypt would ever have this oddly important origin story in common?

The first story tells of the futurist movement founder, Marinetti. In the early 1920s, the Caprese Salad was added to Hotel Quisisana's avant-garde menu for a special get-together of artistic futurists on the island of Capri. Aware of Marinetti's gluten sensitivity, it is said the hotel graciously created a patriotic dish with ingredients that didn't involve pasta, leaving Marinetti duly delighted.

The second tells of a builder from Capri, who locals claim made a light sandwich for his lunchtime break. He grabbed whatever he could find in the fridge along with a few leaves plucked from a windowsill plant, and out the door he went with a kiss to his wife and a "*Ciao, amore*".

In the third, King Farouk of Egypt is said to have visited the beauteous isle in 1951, and the Salad of Capri was presented to him as a tasty snack, allegedly conquering his culinary heart.

When making a Caprese Salad, your basil must be fresh. A sprinkle of oregano will do but mind it won't be called Caprese anymore, if we're getting technical. *Cuore di bue* tomatoes are the chosen ones, prized for their size and flesh. *Cuore di bue* translates as 'beef heart', and we know these large and oddly shaped tomatoes as 'beefsteak'. What makes them so special? The flavour. These tomatoes have very few pips, a firm flesh, and an aromatic flavour which complements the soft, creamy mozzarella just perfectly. If beefsteak tomatoes aren't around, find any large, ripe Italian tomato.

It's not vital that the mozzarella is buffalo or that the tomatoes are beefsteak, but one ingredient that cannot falter on quality is the olive oil. Good extra-virgin olive oil is a must in this humble salad. The bolder, the better.

INSALATA CAPRESE
CAPRESE SALAD

PREPARATION TIME: 10 MINUTES, PLUS 20 MINUTES TO STRAIN THE MOZZARELLA | SERVES 4

INGREDIENTS

250g buffalo mozzarella

2 beefsteak tomatoes

8 basil leaves

Drizzle of extra-virgin olive oil

Sea salt, to taste

OPTIONAL

A drizzle of balsamic vinegar or balsamic glaze

Dried oregano

PREPARATION

1. Strain the mozzarella and let it drain for 20 minutes in a colander. Do this over the sink or a separate bowl to avoid liquid accumulating on the plate.

2. Slice the mozzarella and tomato into equal widths.

3. Arrange the slices with the basil leaves and add a good drizzle of olive oil (and balsamic if you are using it). Serve straight away with a sprinkle of salt and the optional oregano.

COOK'S NOTES

You can use any mozzarella and a selection of different tomatoes. Chop and scatter the tomatoes onto a platter, placing the mozzarella slices and basil leaves on top.

Always take your mozzarella and tomatoes out of the fridge an hour before serving to experience their maximum flavour. Some families keep their tomatoes in a bowl on the kitchen counter so they are always at room temperature – this helps their flavour intensify tenfold.

PROSCIUTTO E MELONE
PARMA HAM AND MELON

Prosciutto crudo, queen of cold meats, is a melt-in-the-mouth, pink, cured pork leg. Lovingly called *'crudo'* for short, the most famed two are San Daniele from northern Friuli and Parma from central Italy, and both are protected geographically.

Crudo di Parma is classically paired with a few things in Italy, and one is melon. There's something about the soft saltiness of the meat striking the crisp sweetness of the melon that is truly sublime. It must be tasted to be believed.

It's a simple *antipasto* but one that works so perfectly that summer in Italy would not be summer without it.

The combination of salty and sweet is a classic one, and some say that, in ancient Greece, Hippocrates dictated the importance of balancing the four elements of nature in foods for optimal health. Water, air, fire and earth; melon is considered opposite to *prosciutto* and therefore its perfect partner.

Who says opposites can't get along?

PROSCIUTTO E MELONE
PARMA HAM AND MELON

PREPARATION TIME: 10 MINUTES | SERVES 8

INGREDIENTS

1 ripe, sweet melon

250g prosciutto crudo (Parma ham), thinly sliced

OPTIONAL

Drizzle of balsamic vinegar or balsamic glaze

PREPARATION

1. Slice the melon into eight equal slices and remove the rind and pips with a small, sharp knife.

2. Wrap slices of ham around each slice.

3. Drizzle with a little balsamic vinegar or glaze before serving, if using.

COOK'S NOTES

Usually, an orangey cantaloupe melon is used, but any sweet melon works well - just make sure it is lovely and ripe.

The flavours of the melon and ham are best at room temperature, so if you prepare this antipasto in advance, keep it covered in the fridge until an hour before serving.

Make sure your balsamic vinegar is aged and flavourful and only drizzle a tiny amount onto each slice.

PRIMI PASTA

LASAGNA DELLA NONNA LILI
NONNA LILI'S LASAGNA

Franceso's *mamma* is a star on the Mangia Mangia menu and in our Italian family. We all agree that she also makes the best *lasagne*. Her unique recipe inspired the beginnings of our small business cooking authentic Italian from our home kitchen when we moved to England. Her beloved Sunday lunch is shared with our customers here in Lichfield and always sells out on the market stall before all our other *lasagne*.

Lasagna is Italian for one pasta sheet and that's why the dish is sometimes called *le lasagne,* but Nonna Lili and most of Veneto know it as *pasticcio*.

There's a bit of a dispute as far as the name and recipe of *pasticcio*, *lasagne* or *lasagna* goes. Ask an Italian in a foreign country facing a menu featuring his homeland dish, and you'll be sure to get a passionate answer. You see, whether *lasagne*, *lasagna* or *pasticcio*, it is an emotional dish - it stirs up memories of busy kitchen tables, rowdy siblings, rumbling tummies, proud mums, good food, and passion. As such, it must be done right.

What makes us long for homemade food is not just the human element. Food is instructions, ingredients and measurements, but it's also flavours, cultures and senses. It's recipes that are handed down through generations, memories, occasions and celebrations. It's floury fingers, high-pitched giggles, licking bowls, stirring pots, and eating sprinkles; it's time spent together in the heart of the home.

A mother's love is more than food, but in Italy, it is where love lies.

LASAGNA DELLA NONNA LILI
NONNA LILI'S LASAGNA

PREPARATION TIME: 15 MINUTES | COOKING TIME: 5 HOURS | SERVES 4

INGREDIENTS

FOR THE RAGÙ

Olive oil, for frying

1 brown onion, peeled and finely chopped

1 carrot, finely chopped

½ celery stick, finely chopped

200g minced pork

200g minced beef

10g unsmoked pancetta
(minced, if possible - see notes)

60g tomato passata

1 cube vegetable or beef stock

125ml milk

¼ tsp grated nutmeg

Dried oregano, to taste

Salt and pepper, to taste

FOR THE LASAGNA

100g butter

100g flour

1L whole milk

¼ tsp grated nutmeg

Salt and pepper, to taste

10 fresh lasagne sheets

100g Grana Padano, grated

125g soft cheese, such as latteria fresco,
moesin or fresh mozzarella (see notes)

PREPARATION

1. Make the ragù the day before by sautéing the finely chopped onion, carrot and celery in a little olive oil until soft (otherwise known as il soffritto).

2. Add the minced meat, including the pancetta, to the pan and brown slightly before adding the passata. Fry for 2 minutes, then transfer to a large pot and add the stock, milk, nutmeg, oregano and pepper and cover with boiling water.

3. Simmer on a low heat with the lid on for at least 4 hours, checking every half hour to see if the water has dried up. Re-cover with boiling water if needed and give the sauce a good stir.

4. After 4 hours, the carrots should be soft and the sauce should be dark and rich in colour. Remove the lid and continue to cook to reduce the ragù until it is nice and thick.

5. Remove from the heat and, when cooled, refrigerate overnight.

6. When ready to assemble and cook the lasagne, preheat the oven to 180°c (160°c fan/gas mark 4). To make the béchamel, melt the butter in a large saucepan and add the flour while stirring with a whisk. Slowly begin to add the milk and keep whisking to ensure no lumps form. Add the grated nutmeg and a pinch of salt and pepper to taste, then continue to add the milk and whisk until it's all incorporated. Simmer on a medium heat, stirring all the time, until the sauce thickens.

LASAGNA DELLA NONNA LILI
NONNA LILI'S LASAGNA

PREPARATION TIME: 15 MINUTES | COOKING TIME: 5 HOURS | SERVES 4

CONTINUED FROM PREVIOUS PAGE

7. To assemble, spread a thin layer of béchamel in a deep dish (about 20x24x8cm), then layer with two pasta sheets placed side by side. Layer with one fifth of the béchamel, one third of the ragù, and a fifth of the Grana Padano, then do the same again to create two layers in total.

8. In the next layer – The Nonna Lili Layer – skip the meat, spread one fifth of the béchamel, layer with your soft cheese and one fifth of the Grana Padano, then add another layer as in step 7 until you reach the top of four layers. Top with the remaining béchamel and Grana Padano.

9. Bake in the oven for 30 minutes and serve hot. Alternatively, you can let it cool and refrigerate it for up to 3 days. To reheat, bake at 180°c (160°c fan/gas mark 4) for 30 minutes, covered. Lasagne freeze well for up to 1 month.

COOK'S NOTES

If you can, ask your butcher to mince the three meats together; otherwise, use finely diced unsmoked pancetta.

Nonna Lili makes a thicker rather than thinner béchamel so that the layers are never sloppy, and she goes quite heavy on the nutmeg. She also chooses fresh pasta sheets, not dried ones. You can cook with dried lasagne sheets, but add an extra 100ml of milk to the béchamel to help cook the pasta.

Nonna Lili uses two cheeses: Grana Padano in every layer for flavour, and a mild, full-fat cheese for the 'Nonna Lili Layer'. If you can't find latteria fresco or moesin, you can use fresh mozzarella, but strain the water 10 minutes before using. Don't be tempted to opt for cheddar or pre-grated mozzarella, as it will never have the right texture.

The creamy cheese goes into the 'Nonna Lili Layer' and never on top. Classic Italian lasagne calls for Grana Padano or Parmigiano to be grated onto a thick layer of béchamel, as this creates the best crust.

Nonna Lili bakes her lasagne the day before and heats them up just before serving - she claims the flavours are better the next day, and the slices always stand up on the plate (as they must!).

Fregona, Veneto

LASAGNA AUTUNNO
AUTUMNAL PUMPKIN LASAGNA

We always get excited when the leaves change, the mists roll in, and the days become chilly. The main reason we rub our hands together gleefully in September is not from the cold but from the thought of autumn's delicious bounty.

In Italy, pumpkin is known as one of the most autumnal of ingredients and can be found in *risotto alla zucca* on most restaurant menus as soon as the seasons shift. Pumpkin gnocchi, pumpkin lasagne, and pumpkin ravioli are all classic *primi* dishes featuring seasonal *zucca* (pumpkin). We have combined its sweet, nutty flavour with salty gorgonzola, walnuts and smoky speck before layering it between fresh pasta sheets and béchamel and baking it as a tasty lasagna.

As an artisan product rooted in tradition, gorgonzola cheese is still made from free grazing on rich pastures, the same as it was centuries ago.

Fertile plains in the region of Lombardy near Milan are famous for cheese-making, and while the origins of creamy cow's milk gorgonzola become hazy around dates and specific origins, they always remain right here. It makes sense that gorgonzola should come from the province of Gorgonzola, but in Pasturo nella Valsassina, just east of Lake Como, a series of perfectly temperature-controlled caves are historically famed for ageing cheese, so some assume the blue-veined beauty was first cultured here during the Middle Ages. That said, Gorgonzola stubbornly lays claim to gorgonzola cheese, so let's leave it at that.

The invention of Italy's favourite blue cheese lies in a charming legend which begs to be told. One thousand years ago, a young, love-struck cheesemaker was busy adding fresh curds to his cheese vat when, due to the distractions of love, he wandered off, forgot the vat, and left the curds unattended and open to the elements. The next morning, feeling more focused, the cheesemaker realised his error, and in a rushed attempt to correct his ways, he threw some extra curds into the mix. Months went by, the cheese aged, and he discovered it had also, surprisingly, changed colour. Intrigued, he then found his 'mistake' rather delicious and made a note of the innovative recipe. Through the power of love and its distractions, gorgonzola was born through a process we know now as *erborinatura*, meaning 'creation of moulds'.

Where would we be without love?

Here's the recipe for Mangia Mangia's most popular seasonal lasagna, which I'm sure you'll also find lovingly comforting as the nights draw in.

LASAGNA AUTUNNO
AUTUMNAL PUMPKIN LASAGNA

PREPARATION TIME: 20 MINUTES, PLUS 30 MINUTES COOLING TIME | COOKING TIME: 1 HOUR 30 MINUTES | SERVES 4

INGREDIENTS

700-800g pumpkin or butternut squash

2 cloves of garlic

4 tbsp extra-virgin olive oil

Salt and black pepper, to taste

200g gorgonzola dolce

¼ tsp grated nutmeg, plus a pinch for the filling

60g speck

100g butter

100g flour

1L whole milk

10 fresh lasagna sheets (if using dried, see notes)

125g fresh mozzarella

30g walnuts, finely chopped

100g Grana Padano, grated

PREPARATION

1. Preheat the oven to 180°c (160°c fan/gas mark 4) and slice the butternut squash or pumpkin in half lengthways. Leave the skin on but remove the pips. Place the garlic cloves (leaving the skin on) into the pip indentations and drizzle 2 tablespoons of olive oil over the pumpkin.

2. Season with a pinch of salt and pepper and cook the pumpkin halves (skin-side down) in a lined oven tray for up to an hour, testing every 20 minutes until soft when poked with a fork. Remove from the oven to cool.

3. When cool enough to handle, scoop the pumpkin flesh from the skin and squeeze the garlic from its skin. Use a handheld blender or a food processor to make a smooth paste using two-thirds of the flesh, the garlic, and half of the gorgonzola together with a pinch of nutmeg and 2 tablespoons of olive oil. Add more oil, if needed, to reach the desired paste-like consistency.

4. Chop the rest of the cooked pumpkin into 1cm pieces. Slice the rind off the speck and dice it into tiny cubes.

5. To make the béchamel, melt the butter in a large saucepan and add the flour while stirring with a whisk. Slowly begin to add the milk and keep whisking to ensure no lumps form. Add the grated nutmeg and a pinch of salt and pepper to taste, then continue to add the milk and whisk until it's all incorporated. Simmer on a medium heat, stirring all the time, until the sauce thickens.

6. To assemble the lasagna, spread a thin layer of béchamel in a deep dish (about 20x24x8cm), then layer with two pasta sheets placed side by side. Spread one fifth of the remaining béchamel onto the pasta, followed by a quarter of the pumpkin paste. Scatter a quarter of the chopped pumpkin, mozzarella and gorgonzola in each layer as well as one fifth of the walnuts, Grana Padano and speck, ensuring you have enough of the latter three for the top. Continue until you have four layers, ending with the lasagne sheets.

7. Finish with the remaining béchamel, Grana Padano and a sprinkling of chopped walnuts and speck cubes.

8. Bake for 30 minutes at 180°c (160°c fan/gas mark 4) and serve hot. Alternatively, you can let it cool and refrigerate it for up to 3 days. To reheat, bake at the above temperature for 30 minutes, covered. Lasagne freeze well for up to 1 month.

Pian di Cansiglio, Veneto

LASAGNA MONTAGNA
'MOUNTAIN' MUSHROOM LASAGNA

It's *mezzogiorno* (midday), and Nonna Lili takes a steaming tray from the oven announcing, "*Ecco, il pasticcio è pronto!*" - "The *pasticcio* is ready!"

In north Italy's Veneto region, where Venice is the capital city, a layered pasta dish is known as *pasticcio*. The rest of Italy may call the same recipe *lasagne*, or *la lasagna* depending on the area; that said, the word *pasticcio* is a fascinating one which describes *pasta al forno*, an oven-baked pasta, with a charming touch of irony.

Pasticcio essentially means 'an ensemble of things', so it describes pies, quiches and even patties, but it also translates as 'a predicament' or 'mess'. For example, you could drop something on the floor and exclaim, "*Ma che pasticcio!*" - "What a mess!"

This perfectly proportioned 'mess' of vegetables and fresh pasta, layered with creamy béchamel and beautiful cheeses might still be classed as '*un pasticcio*'. This recipe has been around since ancient Rome, where it first featured in Latin in Apicio's recipe book, *De Coquinaria*. In here, some 2000 years ago, it had a water and flour crust with a meaty filling.

With the timeless tradition of putting whatever the season brings into a *pasticcio* (or *lasagna*), we are met with all kinds of variants at Nonna Lili's kitchen table and on the Mangia Mangia menu. In autumn, we feature pumpkin, gorgonzola and walnuts in *Lasagna Autunno* (see page 61); in spring, we cook leeks, *prosciutto cotto* and *provolone piccante* into a *Lasagna di Stagione*; and year-round, *Lasagna Montagna* celebrates flavours from the Italian mountains with mushrooms, speck and *scamorza affumicata* (a smoked cheese).

Speck is a product of the lush, mountainous region of Alto Adige, South Tyrol. Bordering Austria and Switzerland to the north, Alto Adige encompasses German, Italian and Ladin culture; both German and Italian languages are studied in schools here and are spoken throughout the region. In Alto Adige, we can clearly note this influence in its architecture, culture and cuisine, and even road signs are bilingual or trilingual.

Speck (German for bacon) is IGP defined and protected geographically. Made exclusively with pork leg from the region, it is brined for three weeks in juniper berries, rosemary and bay leaves, then smoked and matured for about five months. With a smokey, next-level flavour, speck is more intense in colour, texture and taste than prosciutto, and is often added as tiny cubes to pasta, *canederli* (dumplings, see page 123), or gnocchi, and elevates the umami and salty flavours of a dish.

We love the combination of speck, smoked scamorza cheese, and flavourful mushrooms in this Mangia Mangia classic, which also works beautifully as a vegetarian version. Creamy, delicately smoked, and subtle, this recipe is always a triumph with the whole family.

LASAGNA MONTAGNA
'MOUNTAIN' MUSHROOM LASAGNA

PREPARATION TIME: 15 MINUTES | COOKING TIME: 1 HOUR | SERVES 4

INGREDIENTS

180g butter

2 cloves of garlic, peeled and sliced in half

500g chestnut mushrooms, washed and sliced

Dried oregano, to taste

Salt and black pepper, to taste

60g speck

100g flour

1L whole milk

¼ tsp grated nutmeg

10 fresh lasagne sheets (if using dried, see notes)

250g fresh mozzarella (2 mozzarelle)

200g smoked scamorza cheese

100g Grana Padano, grated

COOK'S NOTES

To make a vegetarian version, simply leave out the speck.

You can find sliced speck in some supermarkets or in an Italian deli, sometimes sold in a block. You can use prosciutto crudo as an alternative, but it won't have the same smokiness.

Avoid pre-grated mozzarella because it never gives the right creaminess.

If you prefer to use dried lasagne sheets, add an extra 100ml of milk to the béchamel to help cook the pasta.

Smoked scamorza can be easily found in any good Italian deli.

PREPARATION

1. Preheat the oven to 180°c (160°c fan/gas mark 4). Melt 80g of butter in a wide frying pan and gently fry the garlic until it starts to turn golden. Remove the garlic and add the sliced mushrooms to the flavoured butter with a sprinkling of oregano, salt and black pepper. Cook on a high heat for 5 to 10 minutes, stirring gently until most of the liquid has fried off.

2. Slice the rind off the speck and dice into tiny cubes.

3. To make the béchamel, melt the remaining butter in a large saucepan and add the flour while stirring with a whisk. Slowly begin to add the milk and keep whisking to ensure no lumps form. Add the grated nutmeg and a pinch of salt and pepper to taste, then continue to add the milk and whisk until it's all incorporated. Simmer on a medium heat, stirring all the time, until the sauce thickens.

4. To assemble the lasagna, spread a thin layer of béchamel in a deep dish (about 20x24x8cm), then layer with two pasta sheets placed side by side. Spread one fifth of the remaining béchamel onto the pasta, a quarter of the chopped mozzarella, mushrooms and scamorza, and one fifth of the Grana Padano and speck, ensuring you have enough of the latter two and a few spare mushrooms for the top. Continue until you have four layers, ending with the lasagne sheets.

5. Finish with the remaining béchamel, Grana Padano, a few mushroom slices, and a scattering of speck cubes.

6. Bake in the oven for 30 minutes and serve hot. Alternatively, you can let it cool and refrigerate it for up to 3 days. To reheat, bake at 180°c (160°c fan/gas mark 4) for 30 minutes, covered. Lasagne freeze well for up to 1 month.

Spaccanapoli, Napoli

PACCHERI ALLO SCARPARIELLO
CREAMY TOMATO PACCHERI

Paccheri truly belong to Naples. In harder times, this pasta, also known as *mezze-maniche* (half-sleeves), was a go-to in Neapolitan households. These chunky tubes, whether swimming in sauce or stuffed with ricotta, are always received happily and can easily satisfy the whole family.

Considered part of southern Italy's *cucina povera* food culture, *paccheri* were made cheaply from semolina flour and water. It is said *le mamme* (the mothers) would typically make them on Mondays to use up the weekend's leftover *ragù*, because while other types of *pasta corta* (short pasta) only accompanied their own sauces, *paccheri* suit almost any.

Paccheri comes from the Italian '*una pacca*', or a slap, which you'll understand when you cook with *paccheri*, especially if you make them with one of their most traditional sauces, *sugo di pomodoro* (tomato sauce). The combination of a wide tube of pasta and a liquid sauce means the *paccheri's* distinct slap is heard more than felt, both in the pan and on the plate.

One restaurant – Da Vittorio – has perfected the *paccheri* slap to such a degree that it has become somewhat of an institution, and its customers are not satisfied unless the iconic dish is mixed right beside their table, with the restaurant's signature white bib being supplied especially for the rather messy affair. We're not saying the humble *paccheri* earned Enrico "Chicco" Cerea his three Michelin stars, but it has certainly put Bergamo's countryside restaurant on the *paccheri* map, drawing celebrities from far and wide.

This restaurant's star sauce is none other than Naples' humble *scarpariello*, tweaked into the celebrated *Paccheri alla Vittorio*. *Scarpariello*, named after the *scarpari* (local shoemakers who first made the sauce), sautés the region's fragrant tomatoes in garlic, chilli flakes and extra-virgin olive oil until soft so that the half-done *paccheri* can finish cooking in the pan of sauce. Much like the *mantecatura* of risotto (the process that gives it its creaminess), stir in heaps of basil leaves, *acqua di cottura* (pasta water), and grated hard cheeses like Parmigiano and Pecorino, then keep mixing to create a creamy medley.

The Bergamo brothers, Chicco and Roberto "Bobo" Cerea, add butter, three kinds of tomatoes, and leave out the Pecorino in their restaurant's recipe which is now appreciated as far as St. Moritz, Shanghai and Saigon. Here's my version of the gloriously global *Paccheri allo Scarpariello*.

PACCHERI ALLO SCARPARIELLO
CREAMY TOMATO PACCHERI

PREPARATION TIME 15 MINUTES | COOKING TIME 25 MINUTES | SERVES 4

INGREDIENTS

2 cloves of garlic, crushed

100ml extra-virgin olive oil, plus extra to serve

200g San Marzano tomatoes

150g baby plum or cherry tomatoes

Salt and pepper, to taste

260g paccheri

20g butter

60g Parmigiano Reggiano, grated

15-20 basil leaves, roughly chopped

Dried chilli flakes, to taste (optional)

PREPARATION

1. In a wide, deep pan, sauté the garlic in the olive oil. Chop all the tomatoes into small pieces and add them to the pan.

2. Season with salt and pepper and cook on a low heat for 30 minutes until the tomatoes have softened. In the meantime, put a pot of water on to boil for the pasta. Add a little of the boiling water to the tomatoes if they start to dry up.

3. Blend the sauce with a handheld blender or in a food processor before straining through a sieve. Remove the pips and skin to obtain a smooth consistency, then return the tomatoes to the pan over a low heat and stir in a ladleful of boiling water.

4. When the water is boiling, add the paccheri to the pasta pot and cook for 2 minutes less than the packet states.

5. Strain the pasta, keeping 250ml of acqua di cottura (cooking water) aside, then add the paccheri to the sauce.

6. Mix the butter and grated cheese into the sauce with a wooden spoon, stirring until smooth. Add more pasta water to create a silky sauce, then add the basil leaves, a drizzle of olive oil, the chilli flakes (if using), and keep stirring for 2 minutes. Serve hot!

COOK'S NOTES

Use the ripest tomatoes you can find for the sweetest flavour. Piccadilly work well if you can't find San Marzano. 'Young' Parmigiano Reggiano that has matured no longer than 22 months is creamier in this dish, but Grana Padano is also a good alternative.

Mix continuously while you add the cheese until a smooth sauce is achieved - this is easier if one person sprinkles cheese and the other mixes.

Marina del Cantone, Campania

Via Pescherie Vecchie, Bologna

TAGLIATELLE CON RAGÙ ALLA BOLOGNESE
TAGLIATELLE WITH RAGÙ FROM BOLOGNA

Ragù is essentially a meat sauce with a touch of tomato. The word stems from the French word *ragoût*, meaning stew, but this particular sauce has only been in Italy since tomato seeds were brought to Europe from the Americas on Spanish ships 400 years ago.

Some regions use mince, some use chunks of meat, some pork, some goose, some lamb, some skip the tomato altogether, but the basic concept is simple: create a liquid sauce with a base of onions, celery and carrot (*il soffritto*) and cook it for many hours. Serve with pasta, gnocchi or bread.

Bologna, the capital of Italy's Emilia Romagna region, is considered a major foodie hub where the rules around traditional recipes are very strict. Bolognese (the sauce, not the person) is short for *ragù alla bolognese* (*ragù* from Bologna) and is served with *tagliatelle* or any flat, long pasta, including lasagne sheets (which must be green in Bologna). Contrary to common practice, it isn't served with *spaghetti*, and never *tortellini*, according to the *bolognesi*.

While the rest of Italy make their *ragù* however they regionally choose, Bolognese sauce has been recorded by the Italian Academy of Food since 1982 and is officially made only one way, as are *tortellini bolognesi*. It is considered scandalous in Bologna to add *ragù* to the precious *tortellino*, as it would be to put their sauce onto spaghetti.

'Spag rag' maybe, or perhaps even 'tag bol', but around here... 'spag bol' is not a thing.

Since the region of Emilia Romagna has one of the highest numbers of geographically protected IGP and DOP agri-food products in Europe, who can blame them for feeling entitled to dictate how it's done?

Here's our recipe to make your own *tagliatelle* (with or without a pasta machine). You can also use dried *tagliatelle all'uovo* (egg *tagliatelle*), as most of Italy do, when following these officially protected instructions for Bologna's famous *ragù*.

Making *ragù alla bolognese* the day before is best as its flavours improve with rest. We leave the pot to cool and refrigerate overnight, then give it a good stir in the morning, adjust the seasoning, and cook or freeze it in batches. *Ragù* made the Nonna Lili way (see page 55) is our favourite, but this is the traditional Bologna version, recorded in the Chamber of Commerce, which incidentally is very similar.

TAGLIATELLE CON RAGÙ ALLA BOLOGNESE
TAGLIATELLE WITH RAGÙ FROM BOLOGNA

PREPARATION TIME: 15 MINUTES FOR THE RAGÙ; 1 HOUR 40 MINUTES FOR THE TAGLIATELLE | COOKING TIME: 3 HOURS FOR THE RAGÙ; 20 MINUTES FOR THE TAGLIATELLE | SERVES 6

INGREDIENTS

150g unsmoked pancetta

3 tbsp olive oil, or 50g butter

60g carrot, peeled and finely chopped

60g celery, finely chopped

60g white onion, finely chopped

400g beef, roughly minced

½ glass red or white wine (100ml)

300g tomato passata or peeled tomatoes

Meat or vegetable broth, as needed

Salt and pepper, to taste

200ml full-fat milk

100ml single cream, or more milk (optional)

FOR THE TAGLIATELLE

500g 00 durum wheat flour

5 eggs

5ml extra-virgin olive oil

Coarse salt, for the pasta water

OR 320g dried tagliatelle

Parmigiano Reggiano, grated, to serve

PREPARATION

FOR THE RAGÙ

1. Chop the pancetta into cubes, then finely chop with a mezzaluna knife or similar. Sauté in a frying pan about 25cm in diameter.

2. Add the olive oil or butter and the finely chopped vegetables, then sauté gently until the onion is translucent.

3. Add the minced beef and stir well with a spoon, letting it brown until it sizzles.

4. Add the wine and stir gently until completely evaporated.

5. Add the passata or peeled tomatoes and transfer to a covered saucepan to slowly simmer for about 2 hours. Top up with broth, as needed, so the sauce is always covered.

6. After 2 to 3 hours, taste the sauce, season with salt and pepper and add the milk to balance out any acidity in the tomatoes. Remove the lid and let the sauce reduce until it has a thick, silky consistency.

7. When the ragù is ready, according to Bologna tradition, cream is added if you're using dried tagliatelle. If you are cooking freshly made tagliatelle, it is not necessary.

FOR THE TAGLIATELLE

1. Combine the flour, eggs, and oil until they form a dough. Knead for 10 minutes until it forms a smooth ball. Cover with cling film and refrigerate for an hour.

2. If using a pasta machine, flour a large, clean surface and roll out rectangles of dough, moving down the settings from thicker to thinner, until about 2-3mm thick. Use the tagliatelle attachment to make ribbons, then set aside in nests to dry. If making the tagliatelle by hand, roll out a portion of pasta dough with a wooden rolling pin until 2-3mm thick, dusting with flour as you work. Then, roll the pasta sheet up into a cylinder and slice into 6-7mm-wide ribbons with a sharp knife. Unroll the ribbons and place the tagliatelle in nests on a wide tray dusted with flour to dry a little.

3. Bring a large pot of water to boil and salt the water to taste. Cook the homemade tagliatelle for 2 minutes or follow the packet instructions. You can use a fork to gently separate the tagliatelle in the pot.

4. Strain the pasta and stir in the ragù with a generous sprinkle of Parmigiano Reggiano to serve.

SPECIALITÀ
TORTELLINI

Colombe Artigianali
Senza Conservanti
Durata limitata
Scadenza corta

UNA COLOMBA
E' PRIMAVERA
UNA RONDINE ... NO!

IL REGALO
BOLOGNESE

Please,
facebook
Instagram
#paolotti

ZUPPA
REALE

Paolo Atti e figli, Bologna

VIA DELL' INFERNO

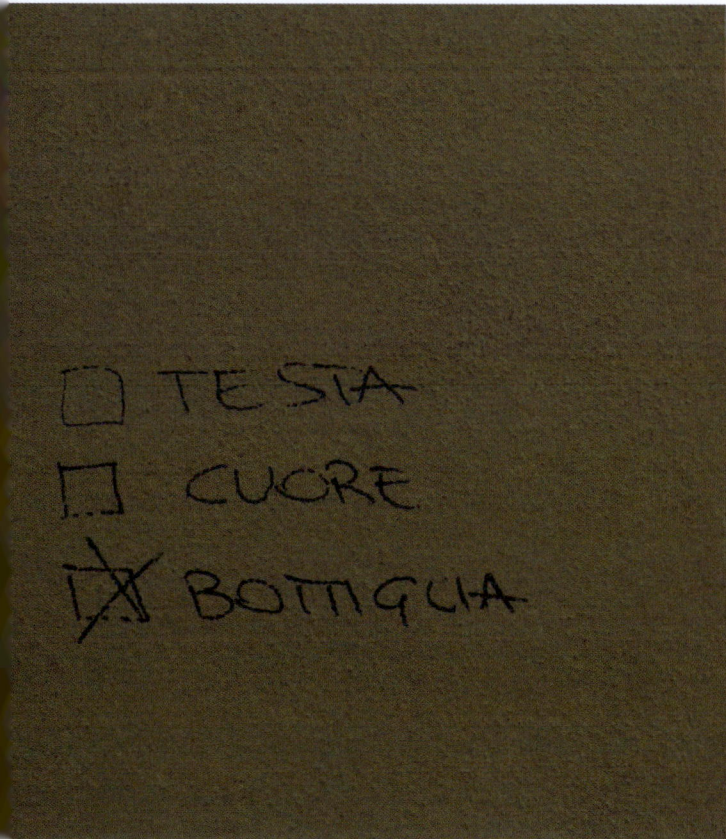

☐ TESTA

☐ CUORE

☒ BOTTIGLIA

Ghetto Ebraico, Bologna

Rione Monti, Roma

VICOLO
DELLE PALLINE
R.XIV

BUCATINI ALL'AMATRICIANA
BUCATINI, THE AMATRICE WAY

A *borgo* is a cherished place, ancient and characteristic; a cluster of homes or a small, stone village where time stands still. In 2001, the tourism council of the *Associazione Nazionale Comuni Italiani*, The National Association of Italian Municipalities, was founded to protect the heritage of these tiny pockets of history. "The Most Beautiful Borghi of Italy" is a renowned list, 300 *borghi* long, featuring some of Italy's most charming settlements, and Amatrice is one of them.

Named The Village of 100 Churches, Amatrice sits in the shadow of the Apennine Laga Mountains within the Roman region of Lazio. The small town suffered a devastating tragedy in 2016 when a terrifying earthquake shook the area, destroying most of the *borgo*, killing 300 people, and leaving over 40,000 homeless. Still reeling from the shock, Amatrice's people are set on rebuilding their hometown slowly but surely, focusing on communal spaces first, and are aided by local Lazio communities and funds from the Eternal City. To welcome the continued stream of visitors who flock to the birthplace of this famous pasta, Amatrice has built a modern, communal catering centre with kitchens to cook school meals and restaurants to serve their namesake dish.

Bucatini all'amatriciana might be labelled 'Roman', but it originated over 100km away on mountain slopes where shepherds would use a skillet to fry *guanciale* for a simple but satisfying 'white' *spaghetti alla gricia*. With the arrival of tomatoes from the Americas in the late 1700s, the local favourite turned *rosso* (red), gaining a drizzle of olive oil and perhaps a chilli pepper too. This version has stolen the spotlight as one of the world's most highly rated pasta sauces.

Made from only a handful of ingredients, the people around Rome proudly state the Pecorino cheese must be local, the *guanciale* never smoked, and the tomatoes San Marzano. They even have a ratio for *guanciale* to pasta, 1:4, to allow the flavours to be properly balanced. If it's not *guanciale*, then technically it's not *all'amatriciana* - of Amatrice.

You can add some chopped onion or garlic, and a little chilli pepper has even made its way into Roman recipes. Most 'long' pasta will do the trick but try to get your hands on proper pork cheek *guanciale* and really good Italian tomatoes - they are the secret to this deliciously simple dish.

Bucatino means 'little hole'. This thick, hollow spaghetti is much-loved in Rome and marries the sauce superbly.

BUCATINI ALL'AMATRICIANA
BUCATINI, THE AMATRICE WAY

PREPARATION TIME: 10 MINUTES | COOKING TIME: 25 MINUTES | SERVES 5

INGREDIENTS

6-7 San Marzano tomatoes, peeled,
or 1 x 400g tinned Italian tomatoes
500g bucatini
Coarse salt, for the pasta water
125g guanciale (cured pork cheek)
¼ glass dry white wine (50ml)
100g Pecorino Romano, grated
Cracked black pepper, to taste

COOK'S NOTES

Bucatini, spaghetti and linguine all work
well in all'amatriciana.

If you are using a chilli, fry it with the
guanciale and remove it from the sauce
before adding the pasta.

If you can't find guanciale at an Italian deli,
seek out a piece of unsmoked pancetta. It
may not have the same flavour or texture,
but it is the next best thing.

PREPARATION

1. Begin by preparing the tomatoes if you are using fresh ones. Blanch them quickly in a pan of boiling water and let them cool before removing the skin and slicing in half to remove the pips.

2. Put a pot of water on to boil for the bucatini and salt the pasta water with the coarse salt.

3. Slice the guanciale into thin strips or chunks and fry directly in a cast iron frying pan or deep skillet without any oil. The fat is released/rendered and will crisp up the meat, making sure it doesn't burn. Add a splash of white wine and remove the guanciale chunks, leaving the fat in the pan. Drip dry and set aside.

4. Put the tomatoes into the hot fat and crush them a little with the back of a spoon.

5. When the pasta water is boiling, cook the bucatini according to the al dente packet instructions; if there aren't al dente instructions, cook for 1 minute less than stated. Strain the bucatini but keep a cup (250ml) of cooking water aside (see 'acqua di cottura' on page 3).

6. Return the guanciale pieces to the sauce and simmer on a low heat.

7. Add the Pecorino to the sauce with a splash of the pasta water, then add the bucatini and stir gently for a minute, being careful not to break the pasta. Add more cooking water if needed to create a silky sauce.

8. Serve hot with extra Pecorino and a twist of black pepper.

CARBONARA ALLA ROMANA
ROMAN CARBONARA

Carbonara is up there with *all'amatriciana* (see page 81), *ragù alla bolognese* (see page 75), *pesto alla genovese* (see page 25) and *arrabbiata*. They're all classic, Italian pasta sauces - some complex, some not, and *carbonara* is not.

You do need to be 'in the know', however, to make proper *carbonara*, so here is our family recipe which is the same for most of Rome.

And can you believe there are only four ingredients?

We all know the importance of beautiful ingredients when it comes to making beautiful food, and Italy is an advocate for ensuring every product is sublime. Yes, you can use bacon, you can even put cream in this – or, heaven forbid, onions – but expect any Roman to tut at your choices, because as world-wide as *carbonara* has become, it's as Roman as Giulio Cesare.

Or is it?

There's an ongoing foodie feud between the capital cities Roma and Napoli; Naples claim they make the best pizza (they also invented it), but Rome say no, they do. Rome has dibs on most things, being the historical and geographical centre of Italy, and they consistently win TasteAtlas' best worldwide city for food, but Campania around Naples wins for the best region.

Rome has laid claim to this pasta sauce too, but unlike *cacio e pepe*, another famous Roman sauce which classically 'belongs' to Lazio (the region around Rome), *la carbonara* only came into play during World War II. Some say it was invented by American soldiers who loved their eggs and bacon, and who asked for the Roman version – *guanciale* – to be added to *cacio e ova*, a cheese and egg pasta from the nearby east-coast region of Abruzzo. Interestingly, *cacio e ova* was made by charcoal-makers (called *carbonai* in Italian, or *carbonari* in Roman dialect).

Some contrarians, however, say that American troops in, you guessed it, Naples, added their K-rations to popular street food spaghetti, and a tasty new dish was born. Perhaps the Romans decided to take rationed powdered eggs and bacon to more appropriate culinary levels and call it *carbonara*?

Who knows, but it is theirs now.

A couple of chefs get very technical about the creaminess of the sauce, so there are two methods to make *la carbonara*: the bain-marie method and the, well, not bain-marie method. Because egg protein starts coagulating at 65°c and stops at 70°c, a thermometer is needed to make sure the cooked sauce is perfectly creamy and not scrambled in the bain-marie. But honestly, nobody bothered with a probe thermometer 70 years ago, so feel free to use the 'not' method which works wonderfully. We have included both for you.

CARBONARA ALLA ROMANA
ROMAN CARBONARA

PREPARATION TIME: 5 MINUTES | COOKING TIME: 30 MINUTES | SERVES 4

INGREDIENTS

400g pasta, such as spaghetti or rigatoni

Coarse salt, for the pasta water

280g guanciale (cured pork cheek)

6 medium-sized egg yolks

200g Pecorino Romano, grated

Cracked black pepper, to taste

COOK'S NOTES

You'll note the creaminess develops from the hot water, Pecorino and egg yolks, so adding pouring cream is not necessary.

Don't be tempted to add egg whites or your carbonara will scramble.

You can find guanciale in specialised supermarkets or delis, but if not, unsmoked pancetta is an un-Roman option, as is Parmigiano Reggiano or Grana Padano instead of Pecorino Romano.

PREPARATION

1. Put a pot of water on to boil for the bain-marie if you are feeling chef-like.

2. Put another pot of water on to boil for the pasta. Adding a pugnetto (about 1 heaped teaspoon per litre) of coarse sea salt to the water is typically advised, but considering Pecorino is quite salty, you can add 1 teaspoon less. Cook the pasta according to the packet instructions.

3. Remove the skin from the guanciale and chop it into cubes or slivers. Fry gently in a non-stick (preferably cast iron) pan until nice and brown. Remove the guanciale and keep to one side.

4. Whisk the egg yolks together in a large bowl and add the guanciale fat from the pan. In the bain-marie bowl (or a bowl on its own), add three quarters of the grated Pecorino Romano as well as a ladle of acqua di cottura (cooking water) and a generous amount of freshly cracked black pepper. Mix well until you have a smooth sauce. Keep warm and continue to test the temperature if you're using the bain-marie method. Keep a bowl of iced water ready if the temperature exceeds 70°c.

5. Drain the al dente pasta, keeping a cup (250ml) of cooking water aside, and while still steaming, add the pasta to the egg sauce, stirring and adding more pasta water if needed until the consistency is as desired.

6. Finally, scatter the guanciale on top with more grated Pecorino and black pepper. Buon appetito!

ORECCHIETTE CON CIME DI RAPA
ORECCHIETTE WITH TURNIP TOPS

The way *orecchiette* stack together is something I absolutely adore, but many Italians claim the best pasta shapes cook uniformly throughout and should never stick.

Formed from water and semolina flour as part of Puglia's *cucina povera* (poor cuisine), these rough-sided, concave discs are fashioned by hand in an instant. All you need is lots of practice.

Walk Bari's beautiful Via delle Orecchiette to spot its women rolling tubes of dough at the roadside on old wooden boards. They slice them into small pieces to be moulded quicky with their thumbs, then throw them onto large drying sieves, where the fresh pasta is then scooped up and sold in bags. Using century-old tools, the women of Bari are keen to tell you all about Puglia's proud heritage while their hands make light work of an age-old tradition.

Puglia, as the heel of Italy, is a region abundantly rich in olives and wine but poor in commerce and industry. In most of Italy, but especially regions like Puglia, when food was expensive and luxuries like cheese were scarce, what could the locals do but reinvent a dish? *Cucina povera* was a movement towards simple, beautiful food that costed less; as such, you'll never find Parmigiano grated onto Puglia's beloved 'little ear' pasta, because dried breadcrumbs – the poorer alternative – are traditionally toasted in olive oil and garlic and sprinkled on top for a delicious crunch.

Per eccellenza, the concave cup of an *orecchietta*, is clearly made to hold its sauce, and here in Bari, there's no sauce more perfect than a simple but tasty green and leafy condiment.

Rapa translates as turnip, but there are many varieties. Perhaps any of these would work, but one that stands out as the *orecchietta's* all-time BFF is *cime di rapa*, or the 'tops of the turnip'.

These essentially refer to the long leaves of the broccoli plant which hide small edible florets amongst them. The whole plant can be eaten, so in winter, when times were hard, farmers would save the 'cream of the *rapa* crop' for exportation and pick the remaining tips of the plants for pasta sauce, while the woodier stems were boiled or grilled.

Throw a couple of local anchovies with garlic, chilli, and Puglia's gloriously fragrant olive oil into the pan and watch how even the poorest of foods and simplest of dishes suddenly come alive.

Here's another thing I love about this - it's quick! The broccoli leaves and florets are cooked in one big pasta pot and then sautéed quickly in the pan, giving you the most gorgeous regional plate of pasta that's ready in no time.

ORECCHIETTE CON CIME DI RAPA
ORECCHIETTE WITH TURNIP TOPS

PREPARATION TIME: 10 MINUTES | COOKING TIME: 20 MINUTES | SERVES 4

INGREDIENTS

1kg broccoli rabe - leaves, tender stems and florets (see notes)

Coarse salt, for the pasta water

300g dried or fresh orecchiette

4 anchovy fillets

2 cloves of garlic, peeled and crushed

4-5 tbsp extra-virgin olive oil

Dried chilies, to taste

OPTIONAL

Breadcrumbs, tossed in olive oil and toasted in a pan with 2 cloves of minced garlic

PREPARATION

1. Rid the broccoli tips of any hard or woody parts and choose the most tender leaves and tips. Chop these into small, uniform pieces and bring a large pot of salted water to the boil.

2. If you are using dried orecchiette, cook as per the al dente packet instructions. If there aren't al dente instructions, cook for 1 minute less than stated. About 6 minutes before straining the pasta, add all the vegetables to the pot.

3. If using fresh pasta, add the leaves and chopped tender stems to the pot of boiling water, and when the water starts boiling again, add the florets and fresh orecchiette directly to the pot.

4. In the meantime, softly sauté the anchovies and garlic in 3 tablespoons of olive oil in a large, deep pan, until the anchovies have disintegrated, then add the dried chillies.

5. Strain the pasta and greens and add everything to the hot pan, tossing the ingredients together on the heat and drizzling over the remaining olive oil.

6. Serve with toasted breadcrumbs for Puglia's authentic version or try a few regional variants by adding fried pancetta lardons or cooked sausage.

COOK'S NOTES

The anchovies can be avoided, but they're there for extra taste, and once dissolved into the oil, they won't bring a fishy flavour to the dish.

If you can't find brocolli rabe, this recipe is just as delicious with tenderstem broccoli.

If you don't love your orecchiette sticking together in little towers (like I do), then simply add a teaspoon of olive oil to the pasta water before the pasta goes in. Italians rarely do this, contrary to popular belief, but when needs must, it is permitted, even by the most traditional of Pulgian mothers.

Buon appetito, amici!

Conca del Sogno, Costiera Amalfitana

FASULARE
2 E

'INI
GRANDI
10 E
AL LO

SGOMBRI
3 EUR
AL LO

GAMBERETTI
FRESCHI
5

SPAGHETTI ALLO SCOGLIO
SEAFOOD SPAGHETTI

Part of the anticipation of going to the beach was delighting in the knowledge of what lunch would bring. While we filled our buckets with sand and stretched our legs in the Adriatic sun, we'd secretly be thinking, "*Cozze o spaghetti allo scoglio?*" – "Mussels or seafood spaghetti?"

Just over the peninsula from Sorrento lies a tucked-away bay whose pebbly beach now buzzes with tourists. It wasn't so well-known once, and local fishermen would haul their boats and daily catch straight up onto the shore between the sunbathers. In the beach-side restaurants, someone setting tables would notice and quickly shout to the chef so he could stroll out into the morning sun for first pick, but no recipes would go through his mind until he'd seen the offerings fresh from the glittering sea. With a contemplative sip of espresso and a scribble on the blackboard – *Il Pescato del Giorno*; Catch of the Day – a dish would be created.

You can find fresh seafood in most Italian supermarkets. There's usually a *banco del pesce* (fish counter), which is quite stunning to behold, especially on Fish Friday. Even though we'd all rather choose and eat the catch of the day fresh from the sea, I encourage you to seek out your local fishmonger or weekly market, or explore the supermarket fish counter, and choose whichever shellfish look the most fresh and delicious for this pasta dish.

Allo scoglio translates as 'from the rocks'. *Scogli* is the Italian word used to describe the shoreline where rockpools form at low tide, and it's where you'll find a natural catch of mussels, clams, octopus, crab and sea shrimp. The beloved *spaghetti allo scoglio* might refer to a collection of these creatures sautéed in tomatoes, white wine and garlic, or perhaps it romantically harks back to the fisherman who'd allegedly boil their molluscs with stones from the *scoglio* to detach them from their shells... *chissà* – who knows? Either way, this dish is delicious.

You can be a little experimental here; our measurements are more of a guide because, in the end, *allo scoglio* is an encompassing idea, enticing you to make the most (and best) of whatever you find.

SPAGHETTI ALLO SCOGLIO
SEAFOOD SPAGHETTI

PREPARATION TIME: 35 MINUTES | COOKING TIME 25 MINUTES | SERVES 4

INGREDIENTS

500g fresh clams, in their shells

500g fresh mussels, in their shells

300g calamari or squid

200g large shrimp

Coarse salt, for the pasta water

5 tbsp extra-virgin olive oil

2 cloves of garlic, peeled and sliced lengthways

250g cherry tomatoes, halved

400g spaghetti

½ glass dry white wine (80ml)

10g flat-leaf parsley, chopped

Cracked black pepper, to taste

OPTIONAL

Dried chilli, to taste

Bread, to fare scarpetta (mop up the juice)

COOK'S NOTES

Linguine is equally glorious in this dish. Any shellfish and molluscs work well too; even a frozen mix works well as a base for fresh mussels and clams. If you are using dried chilli, fry it together with the garlic in step 4.

PREPARATION

1. First, put the clams and mussels into a large pot of fresh water for 30 minutes to release any sand. Debeard the mussels and scrub the shells, if required.

2. Prepare the squid by removing the head and insides, then slice into rings if using whole ones. Clean the shrimp by removing the head, black vein, and shells - you can also leave some whole for decoration.

3. Put a large pot of water on to boil for the spaghetti and season with coarse salt to taste.

4. At this point, heat 3 tablespoons of olive oil in a wide, deep pan and place the garlic cloves into the oil to gently fry on a low heat. Remove the garlic as soon as it begins to turn golden, then turn the heat up to medium and fry the tomatoes in the flavoured oil, along with the squid rings or calamari.

5. When the tomatoes have softened, add the mussels, clams and wine, stirring continuously for a minute. Cover with a lid and leave to simmer for a few minutes so that the shells begin to open.

6. In the meantime, cook the spaghetti according to the al dente instructions on the packet; if there aren't al dente instructions, then cook for 1 minute less than stated.

7. Take off the lid, remove and discard any open, empty shells as well as any that haven't opened, then add the shrimp to the pan and stir in the parsley.

8. When the pasta is ready, strain the cooking water but save a cup (250ml) for later.

9. Put the spaghetti straight into the pan and mix gently, adding some of the cooking water to create a silky sauce. You should already have enough lovely, salty liquid from the mussels.

10. After 3 minutes, crack some black pepper on top and serve right away with a drizzle of olive oil, a scattering of parsley, and some delicious crusty bread.

Lerici, Liguria

TROFIE AL PESTO, PATATE E FAGIOLINI
TROFIE WITH PESTO, POTATOES AND GREEN BEANS

In Italy, we look at a plate of *trofie* and think of one thing: Liguria.

Trofie is the plural for *trofia*, but as pasta dishes contain multiple, most are automatically plural; *spaghetti* – many; *spaghetto* – one; *penne* – many; *penna* – one; and so on.

These simple twists of hand-rolled pasta, shaped thinner at the ends, have traditionally been made by the women of Genova for years. Once rolled exclusively on wooden boards and bare kitchen tables, the art of pasta making used to be as natural as bread-making, but these pasta twists have lived a longer handmade tale than others because, before 1977, they were made completely by hand. The ladies of Liguria would choose a long wooden needle (like a knitting needle) to help form the twist, but besides that, all it took was pure flour, water, and skill. That was until the *simpatico* pasta shape caught entrepreneur pasta-maker sig. Bacci Cavassa's eye as a popular, local food which could be commercialised. In 1977, he made a machine to mass produce *trofie* from his factory, *il Pastificio Novella*, in the coastal village of Sori, which is still active to this day.

The most prized accompaniment to *trofie* is *pesto alla genovese*, but at Sori's yearly feast, *Sagra delle Trofie*, you'll find all kinds of sauces on the menu, including walnut cream, fish sauce and black squid ink.

There's a friendly, ongoing debate in the *trattorie* along the shores of the Golfo Paradiso: "Do you or do you not put green beans in *trofie al pesto*?" It apparently depends on the pasta. Some say that trofie, as a *pasta corta* (short pasta), must only be mixed with pesto, whereas others claim that *trenette*, the local *pasta lunga* (a long pasta, similar to *linguine*), are the best for green beans.

There's no debate at our table - we love them all! Especially this classically Ligurian version mixed with green beans and boiled potatoes; it's another *favoloso* one-pot pasta wonder you can make with our *Pesto alla Genovese* (see page 25).

TROFIE AL PESTO, PATATE E FAGIOLINI
TROFIE WITH PESTO, POTATOES AND GREEN BEANS

PREPARATION TIME: 10 MINUTES | COOKING TIME: 25 MINUTES | SERVES 2

INGREDIENTS

Coarse salt, for the pasta water

120g green beans, washed and trimmed

160g potato, peeled

180g dried or fresh trofie

80g Pesto alla Genovese (see page 25)

Parmigiano Reggiano or Grana Padano, shaved

Extra-virgin olive oil, to serve

PREPARATION

1. Put a large pot of water on to boil and add coarse salt to taste.

2. While the water begins to boil, chop the beans into 2-3cm pieces and the potatoes into roughly 1.5cm cubes.

3. Check the cooking time on the packet of trofie: you need 10 minutes for the vegetables, so if the trofie are fresh, they'll need less cooking time. You can add the beans and potatoes to the water first when it is boiling, then add the trofie later. If the pasta is dried and needs 10 to 12 minutes, put the trofie in the pasta pot first, then add the beans and potatoes after 2 minutes so that everything is ready together.

4. When cooked, strain the pasta water, keeping a cup of acqua di cottura (pasta water) for later.

5. Stir the pesto into the pasta, adding spoons of cooking water to blend it into a silky sauce.

6. Add a few shavings of Parmigiano Reggiano or Grana Padano to your dish with a drizzle of extra-virgin olive oil and enjoy.

PRIMI ALTRI

Borgo Val, Montaner, Veneto

RISOTTO AI PORCINI E SALSICCIA
PORCINI AND SAUSAGE RISOTTO

There's something subtle about risotto. It's not bold nor brash, perhaps reflecting north Italian tastes that lean towards Austrian cooking. In this recipe, butter is used instead of full-flavoured olive oil, and the cheese is milder in taste. Starchy carbohydrates feature the further north one travels in Italy, with risotto embodying the balance of a few key ingredients in one delicate dish. You can taste the rice, the butter, the onions and the broth; in fact, if you ever get the chance, do sample a *risotto alla parmigiana*, parmesan risotto. It may seem bland, like a key ingredient is missing, but in this delicate medley, all ingredients masterfully become key.

In the region of Veneto around Venice, risotto is a much-loved staple that somehow always manages to feel like a celebration. More often than not, it creates an opportunity to showcase the fruits of the season (and region), such as pumpkin and walnut risotto in autumn, asparagus risotto in spring, seafood risotto on the coast, and white truffle risotto in the Piemonte winters.

One of Italy's *risotti per eccellenza* has to be porcini risotto, but foraging for mushrooms is a mysterious art. Our house in Italy sits below a dense, hilly forest where *chiodini (Armillaria mellea)* grow in abundance, but mum's the word in these parts. Early morning in late September, you might notice a silent figure moving among the fields and undergrowth, wicker basket in hand, and eyes cast to the forest floor; it's often the elderly who return to the same prolific spots year after year, hence the secrecy. The joy lies not only in discovering *funghi*, but in the calming art of cleaning them delicately with a blunt knife, perhaps sitting in some September sunshine or beside a warm, wood-burning stove. It may take hours, but herein lies their celebration and value.

A love of nature's bounty, misty mornings, and ongoing tradition becomes woven into a single *funghi* dish. Its product may be a family porcini risotto or *chiodini* with polenta, but that one dish will speak thousands and reflect in the taste and appreciation thereof. You'll find porcini are considered the king of wild mushrooms, and luckily, they are available all year round in dried form. We've featured porcini and locally farmed sausage meat in our Mangia Mangia signature risotto since we first added one to our menu, and it's so wonderfully warming.

Sausage meat is ground coarsely in Italy and breaks up beautifully in a dish, so try to find genuine Italian sausage meat from your deli or local supermarket. Feel free to cook with farm sausages; the rougher and more wholesome, the better.

RISOTTO AI PORCINI E SALSICCIA
PORCINI AND SAUSAGE RISOTTO

PREPARATION TIME: 15 MINUTES, PLUS 4 HOURS SOAKING THE PORCINI | COOKING TIME: 25 MINUTES
SERVES 4

INGREDIENTS

30g dried porcini mushrooms

1-1.5L mushroom broth, boiling (see notes)

80g butter

4 sausages, skins removed

½ clove of garlic, finely chopped

1 white onion, chopped

360g risotto rice

½ glass white wine (100ml)

2 tbsp pouring cream (optional)

Cracked black pepper, to taste

½ tsp dried or fresh parsley

60g Grana Padano or Parmigiano Reggiano, grated

PREPARATION

1. Cover the porcini mushrooms in warm water and let them soak for at least 4 hours (or overnight).

2. Using a slotted spoon, lift the mushrooms from the liquid and chop them into small pieces. Strain the soaking liquid through a sieve to remove any dirt and add it to the mushroom broth.

3. Melt 30g of butter in a deep pan and sauté the sausages, garlic and chopped onion until the onion is soft and translucent and the sausage begins to turn golden. Add the rice to the pan and stir so that it's evenly coated, then pour in the wine.

4. Let the alcohol cook off while stirring gently (for half a minute), then add 400ml of broth.

5. Stir every now and then while the rice cooks on a medium heat, adding another half a cup of broth each time the last is absorbed. Add the cream here, if using.

6. As soon as the rice is al dente, stir in half a ladle of broth and remove from the heat. Using a wooden spoon, stir in the remaining butter, black pepper, parsley and Grana Padano until creamy (see "la mantecatura" in the Cook's Notes). Let the risotto sit for a minute and stir again just before serving.

COOK'S NOTES

Keep a pot of simmering broth beside the pan so you can easily ladle it into the risotto while you cook. You can use porcini stock cubes or make your own vegetable broth by boiling an onion, celery stick and carrot in a large pot of salted water. Ensure it's boiling when you add it to the risotto to avoid slowing the cooking process. Stirring while the rice cooks helps to create a creamy risotto. It is not necessary to constantly stir, just make sure the rice does not dry up and stick to the pan. La mantecatura is the most important part of risotto-making. When you add the butter and Grana Padano at the end, stir vigorously for 30 seconds to create a creamy emulsion from the starch of the rice; this is what makes risotto deliciously oozy.

Cannaregio, Venezia

RISOTTO ALLO ZAFFERANO CON PEPERONI
SAFFRON AND RED PEPPER RISOTTO

Whenever we invite friends over and ask them what we should make, they always say *un risottino*, a little risotto.

While Nonna Lili is famous for her *lasagne*, Francesco is praised for his risotto. With saffron sachets in the cupboard, an onion somewhere around, and arborio rice being a family staple, *risotto giallo* (yellow risotto) often appears on our table.

As we throw on a tablecloth, open a bottle of wine, and chop up some tomatoes for a salad, Francesco gets the red peppers ready in a *soffritto* of onions and butter.

Saffron risotto is a must in Milan, and the iconic *risotto alla milanese* – cooked with bone marrow – can be found on most menus. Typically served '*minimo per due*' – for two people or more – it's often made from scratch. To bring a perfectly cooked risotto to the table in a matter of minutes takes skill and preparation, but there is a trick that Italian restaurants, and Francesco, use to aid the process: creating a base.

Once the initial recipe steps are complete and the rice has been *tosato* (toasted), the cooking process can be halted and resumed once the broth is added. This was the inspiration behind our *risotti* at Mangia Mangia: to offer an authentic dish made from genuine risotto rice.

It may seem simple, but to obtain a creamy risotto is an art. It must be silky but not starchy, and the time between these two delicate phases is a question of minutes. Butter and Grana Padano are added right at the end in a well-known stirring-in process called '*la mantecatura*'. Some chefs insist you must vigorously beat these into the rice with a wooden spoon for at least a minute, and that's a long time to vigorously beat! Half a minute of stirring should give a lovely ooziness to the rice, which is risotto's claim to fame.

The rice you use will determine your cooking time, but there's a rule of thumb that requires a tiny firmness to the centre, like al dente pasta. To obtain this texture, the serving time is crucial; it's a question of practice and knowing your kitchen and your ingredients. There are cooking minutes on every risotto rice box as a guide, but your best gauge is your teaspoon; keep tasting and stop when you think it's almost done. This will allow a few minutes grace for the *mantecatura* and the time it takes to reach the table.

RISOTTO ALLO ZAFFERANO CON PEPERONI
SAFFRON AND RED PEPPER RISOTTO

PREPARATION TIME: 10 MINUTES | COOKING TIME: 25 MINUTES | SERVES 4

INGREDIENTS

0.2g saffron threads (around 2 sachets or half a standard jar)

2 red peppers

80g butter

1 white onion, chopped

360g risotto rice

1-1.5L vegetable broth, boiling (see notes)

2 tbsp pouring cream (optional)

Cracked black pepper, to taste

60g Grana Padano or Parmigiano Reggiano, grated

PREPARATION

1. Soak the saffron threads in 2 tablespoons of hot broth or water.

2. Wash the peppers, remove the pips and stalk, then chop into small pieces.

3. Heat 30g of butter in a large, deep saucepan and fry the onions and peppers until the onion is translucent.

4. Add the risotto rice to the pan and mix so that the rice is evenly coated, la tostatura. After half a minute, add 500ml of broth.

5. Keep stirring gently while the rice cooks on a medium heat, adding 250ml of broth at a time as it absorbs into the rice. Add the cream here, if using.

6. As soon as the rice is al dente, mix in half a ladle of broth and the soaked saffron, then switch off the heat.

7. Using a wooden spoon, vigorously stir in the remaining butter, black pepper and Grana Padano until creamy (see la mantecatura in Cook's Notes). Let the risotto sit for a minute and stir again just before serving.

COOK'S NOTES

Keep a pot of simmering broth beside the risotto pan so you can easily ladle it into the risotto while you cook. You can use stock cubes or make your own vegetable broth by boiling an onion, celery stick and carrot in a large pot of salted water. It is important that the broth is boiling when you add it to the risotto to avoid slowing the cooking process. The quantity needed depends on the type of rice you choose.

Stirring while the rice cooks creates a creamy risotto. It is not necessary to constantly stir, just make sure the rice does not dry up and stick to the pan.

La mantecatura is the most important part of risotto-making. When you add the butter and Grana Padano at the end, stir energetically for 30 seconds to create a creamy emulsion with the starch of the rice. This is what makes risotto deliciously oozy.

RISOTTO COI CARLETTI
FORAGED HERB RISOTTO

One can't help but feel an undeniable love affair with nature while picking through her spring fields of clover and daisies, immersed in *il verde* under a painted sky. Foraging for edible plants is a tradition handed down, and though stemming from a place of hardship, it also celebrates what nature has to offer us, provided we know where to look.

Edible plants are known as '*erbette spontanee*' in Italian, translating to 'spontaneous herbs/grasses'; spontaneous, as in wild.

Every region stocks a pantry of seasonal food, and it goes without saying that the time of year is a determining factor for the bounty. As the ground warms and seeds begin to sprout after winter's freeze, a wide range of forageable plants suddenly appear, making April a busy month of tender buds.

Finding a dish that features *erbette spontanee* on a menu is always a wonderful surprise and a sure sign of a chef who cherishes the food from their land. That said, wild edible plants can also be found for sale in food markets at certain times of the year, whether they're cultivated or harvested wild.

Sciopetin is seeded in our wildflower garden as a springtime favourite, but in order to cook with this wily plant, one must harvest a fair amount, say half a kilogram for a four-person risotto, providing 200 to 300g of *curati* leaves. That's quite a bit of picking, so we traditionally make risotto with wild *sciopetin* foraged from the fields above our house. I love the word *curare* to describe the job of getting food ready to be cooked.

Curare translates as 'to cure' in English, but it also means 'to take care of'. You can *curare funghi* by gently brushing off the soil and trimming any unwanted bits; you can *curare* fish by taking out the innards and descaling the skin; and you can *curare* strawberries by washing them and removing the leaves.

Curare beautifully describes the love and appreciation of good food that we've taken time to harvest, maybe grown ourselves, or found at the market. Usually, it's the elderly *nonne* whose job it is to *curare*. They have time, patience and – most importantly – a chair placed outside in the sunshine.

Only the tender tips from this low woody plant are picked. Once these are washed, the top couple of leaves are blanched in boiling water and kept until needed, or frozen in balls ready for later use. Think of *sciopetin* or *carletti* as a delicate spinach flavour that you might find in *frittata* or *lasagne*, known as *pasticcio* in Veneto.

Sciopetin or *sciopet* derives from *sciopar*, Veneto slang for 'burst', referring to its dainty bell-like seed pods from which its seeds shoot out. Francesco's Venetian grandmother calls them *carletti* in dialect, as in the much-loved regional dish, *risotto coi carletti*. I believe they're called 'Bladder Champion' in English, but the official Latin name is *Silene vulgaris*.

RISOTTO COI CARLETTI
FORAGED HERB RISOTTO

PICKING AND PREPARATION TIME: 40 MINUTES | COOKING TIME: 20 MINUTES | SERVES 4

INGREDIENTS

500g foraged carletti

1 white onion, chopped

80g butter

360g risotto rice

½ glass white wine (100ml)

1-1.5L vegetable broth, boiling (see notes)

Cracked black pepper, to taste

60g Grana Padano or Parmigiano Reggiano, grated

PREPARATION

1. Keep the top four leaves of the carletti with the top shoot and any other leaves below this, then discard the thicker stem. These should weigh 200-300g. Wash in cold water.

2. Sauté the onion in a deep pan with 30g of butter until soft and translucent. Add the rice and pour in the wine once it sizzles. Let the alcohol cook off while stirring gently, then add 500ml of hot broth.

3. Stir in the foraged leaves and keep stirring gently as the rice absorbs the broth. Spoon in more ladles of broth as the risotto cooks to prevent it from sticking to the pan.

4. After about 20 minutes, test the rice by biting into a grain; if it is still hard in the centre, add more broth and stir. Once the rice is al dente, add half a ladle of broth and switch off the heat.

5. Using a spoon, vigorously stir in the remaining butter, black pepper, and Grana Padano until creamy (see Cook's Notes). Let the risotto sit for 1 minute, then stir again before serving.

COOK'S NOTES

Keep a pot of simmering broth nearby so you can easily ladle it into the risotto while you cook. You can use stock cubes or make your own by boiling an onion, celery stick and carrot in a large pot of salted water. It is important that the stock is boiling when you add it to the risotto to avoid slowing the cooking. Stir very gently while the rice cooks. It is not necessary to constantly stir, just make sure the rice does not dry up and stick to the pan. La mantecatura is the most important part of risotto-making. When you add the butter and Grana Padano, stir vigorously for 30 seconds to create a creamy emulsion with the starch of the rice; this is what makes risotto oozy. You can keep the cleaned carletti in the fridge for 3 days, blanche them in boiling water to keep for up to a week, or freeze them for later.

Any foraged herb will work in this humble but deliciously delicate risotto; if you know your wild plants well, feel free to use stinging nettles, wild garlic, or whatever you can safely forage.

Pian di Cansiglio, Veneto

TORTA PASQUALINA
SPINACH AND RICOTTA EASTER QUICHE

Easter Monday is known as *Pasquetta* - Little Easter - in Italy. The traditional thing to do on *Pasquetta* is to go outdoors and have a picnic. There's a saying that goes: "*Natale con i tuoi, Pasqua con chi vuoi*" - "Christmas with your family and Easter with whomever you like". As such, you'll find parks, lakesides, and mountain fields filled with children, friends, and families celebrating spring on this deliciously lazy national holiday.

And what better picnic food than quiche?

Torta Pasqualina, Easter Quiche, was traditionally made by the women of Liguria in Italy's north-western region, around Genova. They would cook beet greens or artichokes for the filling, using whatever else their territory offered in springtime, like marjoram, spring onions and a sour cheese called *prescinsêua*. The special flaky pastry would consist of 33 sheets: one for every year of Jesus's life. Since families shared communal ovens in the 16th century, every family would mark the top of their quiche with a unique symbol. You'll note we suggest using leftover pastry to decorate the top of your Easter Quiche, just like they used to do.

Torta Pasqualina is popular throughout Italy, and not only at Easter. It is also made with savoury Italian shortcrust pastry, called *brisée*, and the filling can be any green, leafy vegetable, or even radicchio. The one characteristic that never changes, however, is the whole baked eggs you'll find inside this *favoloso* quiche when you slice through it.

TORTA PASQUALINA
SPINACH AND RICOTTA EASTER QUICHE

PREPARATION TIME: 20 MINUTES | COOKING TIME: 1 HOUR 10 MINUTES | SERVES 8-12

INGREDIENTS

800g spinach leaves, chard or beet greens

250g ricotta cheese

50g Grana Padano, grated

Nutmeg, grated, to taste

2 sheets of puff pastry

Salt and pepper, to taste

6 eggs, plus 1 egg for the egg wash

COOK'S NOTES

You can experiment with the greens and even use finely chopped artichokes, just as Torta Pasqaulina was once made in Liguria.

I find it nice and easy to use frozen spinach. It can be defrosted in advance so you can put the quiche together quickly. Frozen spinach is also already washed, which is handy.

In Italy, you can find pre-made puff and shortcrust brisée pastry, which are both delicious options for this quiche.

Torta Pasqualina is wonderful when served warm or cold, and it's the perfect pie to make the day before a picnic.

PREPARATION

1. Start by washing the leafy greens in cold water to remove any dirt or bugs, then place them in a large saucepan. Cook on a low heat with the lid on for 10 minutes until the leaves have wilted. Remove from the heat and set aside to cool.

2. Once cooled, squeeze the excess liquid from the greens and roughly chop with a knife.

3. Mix the leaves with the ricotta, Grana Padano, a good grate of nutmeg, salt, pepper, and an egg.

4. Line a 22-24cm diameter baking tin with baking paper and one sheet of puff pastry. Prick the bottom with a fork and pour the mixture into the baking tin, making sure it's spread out evenly.

5. Make five small but deep wells in the mixture with the back of a teaspoon and gently break an egg into each hole.

6. Cover the top of the quiche with the second sheet of puff pastry, folding the edges together to seal the top, then slice a couple of slits into the pastry or prick it with a fork. Add a few decorations using the remaining pastry (cookie cutters work really well).

7. Wash the top of the quiche with beaten egg and bake at 180°c (160°c fan/gas mark 4) for 1 hour. Check every 20 minutes to see if the top is browning too much, and if so, cover with a loose sheet of aluminium foil.

8. Let the quiche cool in the tin until lukewarm, then cut into slices or cool completely for a picnic.

Avelengo, Bolzano

Renon, Bolzano

CANEDERLI TIROLESI
TYROLEAN DUMPLINGS

Just beyond the bustling city of Bolzano, amongst the green hills of Appiano, a recently discovered *affresco* dating back to 1180 is on display within the ancient chapel walls of *Castello Hocheppan*. Depicting the birth of Christ, the *affresco* includes Christ himself, along with Mary, Joseph, and a humble-looking lady.

Possibly a midwife, but known as 'The Watcher', the woman crouches over an open fire with a pan of five dumplings, tasting them with a fork. We frequent this beautiful part of northern Italy often, as our good friend Marika lives in Appiano, and we always look forward to having *canederli* for lunch whenever we visit. Little did we realise how favoured these were until we admired this incredible portrayal of Mary regaining her strength, all thanks to a dish of local dumplings.

Canederli are bread-based; a simple food born from kitchen scraps like *cucina povera*, the cuisine of the poor, and served in twos or threes. The word derives from the German and Austrian '*knödel*' (dumpling), from 'knot' (lump), and although put together from nothing extremely special, they're another example of how the simplest of Italian foods become the most sublime. Originally from Bavaria, the *canederlo* was intended to accompany a meaty stew, but in the northern Italian provinces of Trentino Alto Adige, *canederli* are typically served on their own in broth or butter.

Legend says the humble *canederlo* was once thrown together in desperation by an Alpine innkeeper after a group of 'hangry' mercenaries returned from their pillaging demanding food. With merely stale bread, milk, eggs and leftovers in her kitchen cupboards, the resourceful innkeeper hastily fashioned a plate of delectable dumplings that not only satiated the group of grumpy men but sent them all into a deep and peaceful sleep.

Canederli are traditionally made with bits and bobs from the kitchen, and they're often served as a '*tris*' of three different types. Some of our favourites are green spinach, pink beetroot, and another sumptuous autumnal version featuring porcini mushrooms. This is considered proper mountain food, but it's often fashioned as something more intricate, depending on where you dine, perhaps being served with a crispy slice of pancetta placed on top.

As Alpine food, you'll only find these lovely dumplings north of Venice, and if we may give you a tip... never use a knife to cut *canerderli*, only a fork, or else locals will say it's an insult to the cook.

Here's the innkeeper's famous recipe which we all rely on these days.

CANEDERLI TIROLESI
TYROLEAN DUMPLINGS

PREPARATION TIME: 30 MINUTES, PLUS 2 HOURS 30 MINUTES RESTING TIME | COOKING TIME: 20 MINUTES | SERVES 4-5

INGREDIENTS

300g white bread, diced (can be stale)

225ml milk

3 eggs, lightly beaten

½ tsp salt

¼ tsp pepper

¼ tsp grated nutmeg

60g plain white flour

3 tbsp flat-leaf parsley, finely chopped

200g cheese, diced (like fontina, raclette or gouda), or 80g speck, finely diced

1 white onion, finely chopped

1½ tbsp olive oil

45g unsalted butter

3L vegetable stock

TO SERVE IN BUTTER/DRY (PER SERVING)

20g (1½ tbsp) unsalted butter

1 small bunch of chives or 2 sage leaves, thinly sliced

10g (2 tsp) Parmigiano Reggiano, grated

Cracked black pepper, to taste

TO SERVE IN BROTH (PER SERVING)

250ml vegetable stock

Parmigiano Reggiano, grated

1 small bunch of chives or 2 sage leaves, thinly sliced

PREPARATION

1. Put the bread into a large mixing bowl and add the milk, eggs, salt, pepper and nutmeg.

2. Mix well and leave to rest for at least 2 hours, covered with a tea towel, in a cool place or in the fridge. Stir occasionally to ensure that the bread absorbs the liquid uniformly.

3. After 2 hours, add the flour, then stir in the parsley and cheese or speck.

4. Fry the chopped onion in the oil and butter for 10 minutes on a medium heat, stirring occasionally. Let the onion cool, then stir it into the bread mix.

5. Let the mixture rest for another 30 minutes, covered with a tea towel. It should look uniformly moist and slightly sticky.

6. Using your hands, form the canederli by pressing together enough mixture to make balls, 60 to 80g each. You should be able to make 12 to 14 balls.

7. Roll each ball in plain flour to seal the outside and prevent the canederli from sticking to each other. When all the canederli have been dusted, re-roll them in flour and compress them a second time.

8. Ready the vegetable stock by bringing it to the boil. Gently lower the canederli into the pot with a slotted spoon, bring to a gentle boil once more, then cook the canederli for 12 to 15 minutes (they should float the whole time). When ready, gently lift them out.

9. If serving the canederli 'dry', warm the butter just enough to melt it. Place three canederli onto each plate and pour the melted butter over them. Finish with a sprinkle of thinly sliced chives or sage leaves, grated Parmigiano and freshly ground black pepper.

10. If serving the canederli in broth, prepare a separate pot of vegetable stock and bring to the boil (as the one used for boiling the dumplings will be cloudy from the flour). Place two or three canederli into a bowl and pour over the hot broth. Finish with grated Parmigiano and finely chopped chives or sage leaves.

Montaner, Veneto

GNOCCHI BURRO E SALVIA
GNOCCHI WITH SAGE AND BUTTER

Venerdì Pesce, Giovedì Gnocchi. Fish Friday, Gnocchi Thursday.

This is a firm family favourite, and if you have sage growing nearby, even better - you only need a few leaves to deliver all the flavour. With a distinctive fragrance that typically suits meaty dishes, sage equally shines in this beautiful, vegetarian *primo* (first course).

We rarely make gnocchi from scratch because there are a range of versions readily available, with my absolute favourite being pumpkin gnocchi. I know many Italian mums would never dream of buying gnocchi, and they'd try relentlessly to convince me to make them fresh, saying it's as easy as pie. They'd say: "You can make a big batch of gnocchi. They freeze well and can be cooked from frozen for an easy meal. There's no reason not to!"

Rumour has it, the trick to gnocchi that don't fall apart is the type of potato you use. Some swear by *farinosa*, floury potatoes, while others swear by waxy. We use white potatoes, and they always do the trick.

Homemade gnocchi are soft, special, and delicious - there's no doubt about it. You don't need anything particularly complicated to bring some floury fun to the kitchen on a dreary day. Just potatoes, flour and an egg will have children happily rolling out gnocchi sausages, and they can even get fancy with a fork or wooden gnocchi board. What's better than homemade gnocchi for dinner when all is cleared away?

There are so many sauces to accompany the fluffy potato pillows we all know and love - gorgonzola or *quattro formaggi*, four cheeses, is *favoloso*, as is *ragù* (see page 75), and you can't go wrong with a simple *sugo di pomodoro*, tomato sauce. This particular recipe is a classic and is often offered in Italian restaurants to children who are undecided about the menu. *Ricotta affumicata*, smoked ricotta, is tricky to find outside of Italy, but if you spot it on a cheese counter, grating some on top of this dish will bring the most wonderful intensity. Grana Padano is what we always have in the fridge, which is equally delectable, and then I like to fry a few extra sage leaves to crisp up as a lovely little bit of crunch for the plate.

While Friday is for eating fish, Thursday is 'Gnocchi Day' in Italian pasta shops, so here goes: today we're making gnocchi.

GNOCCHI BURRO E SALVIA
GNOCCHI WITH SAGE AND BUTTER

PREPARATION TIME: 50 MINUTES | COOKING TIME: 10 MINUTES, PLUS 30 MINUTES IF MAKING GNOCCHI FROM SCRATCH | SERVES 3-4

INGREDIENTS

80g butter

4 tbsp extra-virgin olive oil

12 sage leaves

600g gnocchi (for homemade, see below)

Cracked black pepper, to taste

30g ricotta affumicata (smoked ricotta), Grana Padano or Parmigiano Reggiano

FOR HOMEMADE GNOCCHI

500g white potatoes

1 egg

125g strong bread flour or 00 pasta flour

¼ tsp grated nutmeg (optional)

½ tsp salt

COOK'S NOTES

Freeze gnocchi on a sheet of parchment paper and, once frozen, keep in sealed bags for 1 month to be cooked straight from frozen. They only last a day in the fridge, so I always recommend freezing them.

PREPARATION

1. To make the gnocchi, boil the potatoes (with the skins on) in a large pot of water for 20 to 30 minutes until cooked through and soft when poked with a fork.

2. Remove the skins when the potatoes are cool enough to handle and use a passaverdura, vegetable mill, or ricer to create a smooth consistency. You can also use a potato masher; just make sure there are no lumps.

3. While the potato is still warm, work directly on a clean surface or in a large bowl to mix in the egg, flour, salt and nutmeg. Knead for a few minutes to create a smooth, soft dough.

4. Dust another clean surface with flour and roll out long sausages of dough, roughly 2cm thick, with your hands. Using a sharp knife or dough cutter, slice 2cm shapes and form them into pillows with your fingers. You can also use a gnocchi board or fork to form grooves in each one with a downward sliding motion. This takes a bit of practice, but there's no need for perfectly shaped gnocchi, as long as they are more or less the same size.

5. Bring a large pot of salted water to the boil to cook the gnocchi later.

6. To make the sauce, melt the butter into the oil in a deep saucepan. Add the sage leaves and gently fry on a very low heat, making sure to move the pan off the heat if the butter begins to brown. After 2 minutes, remove the sage and let it drain on a sheet of kitchen paper towel. If you love crispy sage leaves, let them toast a little longer in the butter.

7. Tip the gnocchi into the boiling water and wait a few minutes until they rise to the top. Scoop the gnocchi from the pot with a slotted spoon or spider sieve and add them into the pan with the sage butter. Gently stir to coat.

8. Place the gnocchi into bowls with the butter, sage leaves and a sprinkling of black pepper and grated ricotta, Grana Padano, or Parmigiano.

Monte Rajoc, Veneto

SPÄTZLE AGLI SPINACI
SPINACH SPÄTZLE

Spätzle, or spaetzle, are a traditional German noodle with a wide-reaching popularity that spreads as far as Hungary and France. Having made their way into Italy's north-most Trentino Alto Adige provinces which border Austria and Switzerland, this dish now forms part of Tyrolean food culture, too. In Germany, these wheat noodles are often cooked to accompany meaty stews as a 'white' version made with cheese. In northern Italy, spätzle are generally made from spinach and served 'green' as a *primo*, the culinary step between starter, *antipasto*, and main, *secondo*.

While spätzle's traditional sauce is cream and speck, as shown here, another favourite is crispy pancetta or ham with melted butter, a scattering of sage leaves or chopped chives, and a generous grating of Parmigiano.

We enjoy spätzle often, finding packets in supermarkets which are conveniently ready to tip into a pan and cook directly in a sauce. Luckily, these tasty egg noodles are also easy to make from scratch, even without a spätzle-maker.

Most Tyrolean kitchens stock a specialised spätzle tool to slide the batter back and forth over a pot of boiling water, making light work of a preparation process which is to their family lunches as Nonna Lili's *lasagne* are to ours (see page 55). A simple yet effective method, if you do not own a spätzle-maker, is to find a colander with holes large enough to allow the batter to drop through and form the noodle shapes. Otherwise, an even simpler method is to flick thin sections of batter from the edge of a bowl straight into the pasta pot. The kitchen may become slightly green and sludgy, but spätzle are hard to get wrong and worth every effort.

Sometimes called *gnocchetti tirolesi*, little Tyrolean gnocchi, these are fun to make, just like potato gnocchi (see page 123), and can also be prepared in advance. In a country that spans from snowy ranges in the north to dry coastlines in the south, we look forward to spätzle as 'mountain' food, reminiscent of the clear Alpine sunshine and high Dolomite peaks. To savour this dish, chop up a cabbage salad (see page 181), pour yourself a cold pint, and find a spot in some bright sunshine. Perhaps you can hear a faint jingling of cow bells in the distance, if you listen hard enough.

Buona montagna.

SPÄTZLE AGLI SPINACI
SPINACH SPÄTZLE

PREPARATION TIME: 20 MINUTES PLUS 30 MINUTES TO STAND | COOKING TIME: 15 MINUTES | SERVES 4

INGREDIENTS

300g spinach, blanched (or frozen spinach)

2 eggs

250g strong bread flour or 00 pasta flour

¼ tsp grated nutmeg

¼ tsp salt

150ml water (see notes)

80g speck or smoked pancetta

30g butter

250ml single cream

Coarse salt, for the pot

30g Grana Padano, grated (optional)

Cracked black pepper, to taste (optional)

COOK'S NOTES

The amount of water you add to the batter in step 2 depends on the spinach you use. You are looking for a pancake batter-like consistency. Feel free to add however much you need for the batter to easily fall through the holes.

PREPARATION

1. If using frozen spinach, defrost it first and squeeze out any excess water. Then, add the spinach to a food processor or blender and blitz to form a purée. If more liquid is required, simply add one of the eggs.

2. Transfer to a bowl and add the (rest of the) eggs to the spinach, followed by the flour, nutmeg, and salt, and begin to stir in the water, a little at a time, to create a gloopy batter. Work for a few minutes, then let the batter rest, either covered in the fridge or in a cool spot, while you prepare the sauce.

3. Discard the rind from the meat then slice it into thin 2cm ribbons or tiny cubes.

4. Heat the butter in a wide, deep saucepan and gently fry the speck or pancetta until crispy.

5. Scoop out the speck and put it to one side, then pour the cream into the pan and switch off the heat.

6. Heat a large pot of salted water and prepare a metal colander with holes around 8mm wide (unless you own a special spätzle-maker). Prepare a bowl of cold water and ice on the side.

7. Use your spätzle-maker or place the colander on top of the pasta pot and, with the back of a spoon, push the spinach mixture through the holes so small amounts plop into the boiling water. You could also use a soup spoon to flick small slivers of batter from the edge of the bowl directly into the boiling water.

8. Every minute or so, with a slotted spoon or spider strainer, scoop up the cooked spätzle (those which have risen to the top) and place them into the ice water to halt the cooking process. Work in batches until all the mixture is cooked.

9. Warm the cream and add two thirds of the meat to the pan, then strain the water off the cooked spätzle and combine with the sauce. Mix well and plate up, finishing with a sprinkling of meat, a grating of cheese, and some cracked black pepper.

SECONDI

Citta'Vecchia, Trieste

SPEZZATINO
BRAISED BEEF STEW

There's something primally satisfying about a stew bubbling on the stove, and the beauty of any stew is using up what you have. Most meat, if cooked slowly and long enough, becomes deliciously soft and tasty. This recipe does take time but it's one of those meals that can simply do its thing while you're busy doing other things.

The custom of serving *spezzatino* with polenta is not just a north Italian tradition. Polenta is a staple in most Italian larders due to its incredible versatility. North Italian people are nicknamed '*polentoni*' by those south of Rome because, in the northern regions of Veneto, Piemonte, Lombardia and anywhere in the Alps, polenta is a firm favourite in home kitchens and on restaurant menus. You can bake, fry and grill polenta; *infatti*, it never goes to waste because 'proper' polenta takes a good hour to make, so when you make a pot, you make a big pot and keep the leftovers for polenta slices.

There are two main types of yellow polenta: the traditional one and the instant one, also called *polenta lampo*, or lightning polenta. They are made the same way, but one takes roughly an hour, while the other takes roughly 5 minutes. It may seem like a no-brainer, but you'll notice the difference in texture, with traditional polenta being much creamier and softer.

In Italian delis or specialised shops, look out for variants of traditional polenta, such as ones made from nutty and wholesome ancient grains like *saraceno* (buckwheat), or white polenta, which is used in Venice's most popular regional delicacies.

Instead of polenta, mashed potato or thick slices of crusty bread both make lovely bases to soak up the wonderful sauce in this *spezzatino*.

SPEZZATINO
BRAISED BEEF STEW

PREPARATION TIME: 15 MINUTES, PLUS COOLING OVERNIGHT | COOKING TIME: 2 HOURS | SERVES 4

INGREDIENTS

5 tbsp olive oil

1 brown onion, finely chopped

1 celery stick, finely chopped

1 large carrot, finely chopped

600g braising steak, cut into 3cm chunks

40g plain flour

¼ glass dry white wine (40ml)

750ml beef stock, plus extra boiling water

Cracked black pepper, to taste

2 sage leaves

1 bay leaf

1 sprig of rosemary

1 tsp coarse sea salt

375g polenta flour (instant or traditional)

OPTIONAL

2 tbsp tomato passata (see notes)

PREPARATION

1. To prepare the soffritto, heat a deep braising pan with 3 tablespoons of olive oil and add the vegetables. Cook on a medium heat until the onion is translucent. While the vegetables are cooking, dust the chunks of beef with flour so they are lightly coated. Shake off any excess flour.

2. Turn to a medium-high heat then add 2 tablespoons of olive oil and the beef chunks. Fry while stirring gently, removing any sticky bits from the pan edges with a wooden spoon to make sure nothing burns. A lovely, golden crust in places is welcome, as this is what brings the flavour.

3. After a few minutes, add the wine and scrape down the sides of the pan. When the wine has been absorbed, add the beef stock. The liquid will cover everything and might seem too much but will cook down to create a delicious sauce.

4. Season with black pepper and add the herbs, then cover and simmer gently for 1 and a half hours. Check every 20 minutes to ensure no meat is sticking to the pan and the liquid has not dried up. If it does stick, loosen the meat by removing the pan from the heat for 5 minutes – you'll notice the meat will soften and become easier to scrape down the sides. Keep adding boiling water to cover the ingredients and cook until you can pull the meat apart with a fork. Remove the herbs and check the consistency – you can cook it without a lid for a few minutes if you want a thicker sauce. Cool and refrigerate overnight in a sealed container.

SPEZZATINO
BRAISED BEEF STEW

PREPARATION TIME: 15 MINUTES, PLUS COOLING OVERNIGHT | COOKING TIME: 2 HOURS | SERVES 4

CONTINUED FROM PREVIOUS PAGE

5. The next day, if making traditional polenta, begin 45 minutes before reheating the spezzatino. Start by boiling 1 and a half litres of water in a heavy-bottomed saucepan (preferably copper) and salting the water with a teaspoon of coarse salt. If you are using instant polenta, review the timing on the packet instructions, and start the same way but only when about to reheat the stew.

6. Pour the polenta in a steady stream, a pioggia, into the simmering water while whisking to prevent lumps forming. Keep mixing until the polenta thickens — at this point, you'll need to switch to a wooden spoon. Cook on a low heat and give it a good stir every 10 minutes. Don't worry if a crust forms on the sides of the pan with traditional polenta, as this is normal. Word on the street is, when it's ready, the crust will pull away from the pan, but you can taste it after 40 minutes to see if the consistency is creamy (and adjust the seasoning, too, at this point). Some families stir in a knob of butter at this stage, and you can add more boiling water if you'd prefer a smoother texture.

7. Once ready, serve immediately before the polenta solidifies with a large ladle of spezzatino on top.

COOK'S NOTES

Feel free to use red or white wine in the spezzatino.

Where we live in Veneto, spezzatino is made with a splash of passata. If you'd like to use tomato, you can add it in step 5.

We always make spezzatino a day ahead so the flavours have time to improve. It freezes very well for up to 1 month.

Missiano, Bolzano

Cannaregio, Venezia

POLPETTE VENEZIANE
VENETIAN MEATBALLS

Rialto Bridge in Venice may seem like the perfect spot to take your Grand Canal snap, and indeed it is very beautiful around here, but for us, the area of Rialto carries extra clout due to the sheer number of *bàcari*.

According to ancient tales, the word *bàcaro* originates from the Venetian expression '*far bàcara*', meaning to celebrate in the name of Bacco, God of Wine. As expected, a Venetian *bàcaro* is traditionally frequented by locals, at absolutely any time of day, for a tumbler of wine they call *n'ombra de vin*. While meals in Italy tend to have a more specific order, over in Rialto, a bracing grappa with your first coffee or an early-morning prosecco and *polpetta* at the market are always warmly welcomed.

Next time you're in Rialto, step back in time at one of Venice's *bàcari* for a snippet of easy-going, local tradition. The best time of day is 'Aperitivo Time', an hour or so before dinner, when the little places bustle with loud conversations that spill out onto the streets. Their brick walls, marbled Venetian floors, bare wooden tables and counters packed full of *cichetti* (appetisers) are easy to spot.

Venice prides herself on 'lagoon food', served up as small, enticing snacks to accompany a glass of wine. There are many traditional types of *cicchetti* we always expect to find, like *sarde in saor* (sardines), *baccalà mantecato* (stockfish), and *polpette* (meatballs). With a love of good food and flavour, you'll find that a *bàcaro's* host loves to put their twist on tradition and will proudly go through what's on offer.

It's hard to say which *bàcaro* makes the best *polpetta*, but most Venetians will automatically point out Alla Vedova just off Strada Nova. We were first brought here by our friend Andrea to taste "The best meatballs in Venice", all for the modest price of 1 euro each. Granted, this was 20-odd years ago, but the tradition continues to grab a glass of wine and a meatball and stand outside until it becomes a bit of a street party. Just inside the *bàcaro* door, situated in a tiny, unassuming alley, freshly made *polpette* are placed onto the *cicchetti* counter and fly away on paper napkins. With one hand holding a meatball, the other is free to hold a wine tumbler.

Follow the sound of clinking glasses to find one of the many *bàcari* in the area. Try Al Ravano, De Bischeri and Do Mori over the bridge near the Rialto market, where Casanova supposedly took his 132 lovers for their first dates. The *polpette* over there must've been quite something!

Our family recipe is just as popular, and eyes literally light up when the question, "What's for dinner?" is answered by "*Polpette*".

Bacaro al Ravano, Venezia

Campo San Polo, Venezia

POLPETTE VENEZIANE
VENETIAN MEATBALLS

PREPARATION TIME: 40 MINUTES | COOKING TIME: 30 MINUTES | SERVES 3-4

INGREDIENTS

80g white bread

250ml milk

300g minced pork

1 egg, beaten

2 tbsp dried parsley, or 1 handful of fresh flat-leaf parsley, finely chopped

30g Parmigiano or Grana Padano, grated

Pinch of ground nutmeg

½ tsp salt

Cracked black pepper, to taste

30-50g breadcrumbs

Sunflower oil, for frying

PREPARATION

1. Break the bread into chunks and cover with the milk. Leave to soften for at least 20 minutes.

2. When the bread has absorbed the milk, mash it with a fork so there are no big lumps and squeeze out any excess liquid through a sieve.

3. Add the rest of the ingredients, excluding the breadcrumbs and oil, and mix well.

4. Using your hands, form balls, roughly 60g each, by rolling them in your palms. Roll each ball in breadcrumbs as you make each one.

5. When all the meatballs are ready, fill a deep frying pan, 1.5cm deep, with sunflower oil.

6. Fry a batch of meatballs on a medium heat, turning each one over when the meat inside begins to lighten, about 5 to 10 minutes each side.

7. Break open the thickest meatball to ensure it is cooked through, then remove them with a slotted spoon and place on kitchen paper to absorb any excess oil. Serve warm.

COOK'S NOTES

You're welcome to add a clove of crushed garlic or finely chopped onion, as well as use beef mince instead of pork.

Another local variation is tuna instead of meat, which is also delicious.

The ground nutmeg can also be excluded if you aren't a fan.

TAGLIATA
SLICED STEAK

I've found food takes up a considerable amount of thought and time in Italy. As the beautiful subtext of so many conversations, it seems we're always thinking about what we're eating, where it comes from, and who made it. In our household, we openly discuss how delicious our meal is and what could make it better. Sitting around a table, in true Italian style, we're already considering what we'll be having for the next meal while we're still enjoying the current one.

In a culture with this much focus on good food, the joy of growing, producing and preparing it really shines through, and I truly believe you can taste it.

I've also noticed in Italy, where so much care is taken to produce beautiful ingredients, that adding a sauce can be thought of as offensive. Your *Cozze alla Marinara* (see page 157) might be served with a slice of lemon, but you are not expected to squeeze it. According to their culture of good food, if the fish is fresh, nothing needs to be added except a drizzle of fine olive oil and a seasoning of salt and pepper. Same goes for steak; same goes for potatoes. The only 'sauces' you're likely to find in an Italian kitchen are ketchup and mayonnaise, but these are reserved for chips or combined and served as a pink sauce (named *salsa rosa*) to accompany a toasted sandwich.

La Tagliata is a simple dish of sliced steak on a bed of rocket – not even Grana Padano is really essential. The chosen cut is usually *entrecote*, rib-eye, but any boneless steak can easily be grilled or fried for this marvellous main course. It only calls for good quality olive oil and the best beef you can find.

Always cooked medium rare and served as the name states – 'sliced' – this is an all-year round favourite that was purportedly first mastered by a Tuscan chef in Pisa, who had been inspired by the classic *fiorentina*, Florence's hefty beef steak.

TAGLIATA
SLICED STEAK

PREPARATION TIME: 5 MINUTES, PLUS 1 HOUR TO REST | COOKING TIME: 10 MINUTES | SERVES 2

INGREDIENTS

450g entrecote, rib-eye or sirloin steak

3 tbsp extra-virgin olive oil, plus extra to serve

30g rocket leaves, washed

Salt and pepper, to taste

25g Parmigiano Reggiano or Grana Padano, shaved

OPTIONAL, TO SERVE

Cherry tomatoes, halved

Aged balsamic vinegar or glaze

PREPARATION

1. Remove the steak from the fridge an hour before cooking to allow the meat to reach room temperature.

2. Pat the meat dry with kitchen paper and rub it with olive oil.

3. Heat a griddle pan until scalding hot, or place a grid over a bed of hot coals and lay the steak on top. Reduce the heat and cook for 2 to 4 minutes on one side.

4. Meanwhile, lay the washed rocket on a platter or wooden board, dress with balsamic vinegar or glaze, and season with salt and pepper. Scatter the tomatoes over the top, if using.

5. Turn the steak and season the cooked side with salt and pepper. Cook the other side for another 2 to 4 minutes, then place onto a board, season with more salt and pepper, and cover loosely with foil. Let the steak rest for 1 minute.

6. Slice with a sharp knife and place the slices onto the bed of rocket. Cover with Parmigiana shavings, drizzle with olive oil, and serve.

FILETTO DI PESCE ALLA MEDITERRANEA
MEDITERRANEAN FILLET OF FISH

The word 'Mediterranean', for me, conjures up dry coasts and waves breaking onto pebbled beaches; windswept, bare outcrops and low, scraggly shrubs that cling to the rocks. Buzzing cicada song and a gentle sea breeze meet in this fish dish, and though it might simply be a medley of herbs you love, scattered with onion or garlic and tomatoes, my Mediterranean is oily olives and salty capers. Feel free to substitute these with sun-dried tomatoes or grilled peppers, if you like.

We are big tomato fans in our family. They appear at breakfast, chopped with olive oil and salt beside a piece of toast. They feature in pasta sauces at lunchtime and again for dinner as a side salad, as well as in a main course like this baked fish fillet.

Seek out the full flavour of the very best tomatoes and do what many Italian families do: keep them in a bowl on the kitchen counter instead of in the fridge. The taste improves so much.

The fish fillet can be any white fish - cod, haddock, mackerel or sea bass, and this recipe even works beautifully with frozen fillets, which are easy to find in your local supermarket. Defrost them first, drizzle with olive oil, and dress with the Mediterranean ingredients before oven-baking.

Fresh thyme, oregano, parsley, and even rosemary work well in this dish, but flat-leaf parsley is a go-to in Italian kitchens. Albeit very pretty, the curly variety is used more as a garnish than in cooking. Parsley is loved in so many Italian meals and becomes an essential ingredient in recipes like Borlotti Bean and Onion Salad (see page 193), or Lemon Pesto (see page 21). It's particularly prized in fish and seafood dishes due to its fresh flavour.

Oregano and thyme are hardy plants that grow wild in arid, rocky Mediterranean climates. In Italy, oregano is appreciated for its perfect harmony with tomato, much like basil is. In this dish, thyme, oregano and marjoram all bring their fragrant oils to the plate.

Rosemary grows wild along the roads in coastal Europe as a low, creeping shrub. Its medicinal, herbal flavour can be strong, but it's wonderful paired with olives and tomatoes. I love to scatter its lilac-coloured flowers onto cakes, and they would be beautiful here sprinkled over the fish fillets just before serving,

FILETTO DI PESCE ALLA MEDITERRANEA
MEDITERRANEAN FILLET OF FISH

PREPARATION TIME: 10 MINUTES | COOKING TIME: 25 MINUTES | SERVES 2

INGREDIENTS

3 tbsp extra-virgin olive oil

2 fillets white fish, skin on (like cod, haddock, sea bass or mackerel)

2 spring onions, ½ red onion, or 2 cloves of garlic, finely sliced

1 handful of cherry tomatoes, halved

1 small handful of pitted olives, halved

10-15 capers

2 tbsp flat-leaf parsley, fresh thyme, oregano, rosemary or marjoram leaves, chopped

Salt and black pepper, to taste

PREPARATION

1. Preheat the oven to 220°c (200°c fan/gas mark 7) and prepare a baking dish large enough to fit the fillets side by side. Drizzle with a teaspoon of olive oil to coat the base of the dish.

2. Lay the fish fillets in the ovenproof dish and cover with the rest of the ingredients.

3. Bake for 20 to 25 minutes until cooked through. Test the thickest part of the fillet with a fork to check if the flesh breaks easily, then remove from the oven and serve with some seasonal vegetables and Fagioli Borlotti con Cipolla (see page 193).

COOK'S NOTES

You can substitute fresh fish for frozen but defrost it completely in the fridge before cooking.

Praiano, Salerno, Campania

Lerici, La Spezia, Liguria

COZZE ALLA MARINARA
MUSSELS MARINARA

Mussels are one of the simplest seafoods to prepare. They're easily and inexpensively found and make a wonderful *antipasto*, but we love them as an abundant main course with lots of bread to soak up their salty juices.

Marinara means 'of the sea' but generally refers to a style of Mediterranean cooking which widely incorporates herbs like basil or oregano with fragrant olive oil and tomatoes. The two most classic of all *pizze*, earning first place on each Italian pizzeria menu, are *pizza margherita* and *pizza marinara*. Naples is home to *pizza margherita*, and in the city's iconic Antica Pizzeria da Michele, only three *pizze* grace the menu: *Margherita* - tomato, *mozzarella di bufala* and basil; *cosacca* - tomato, Pecorino and basil; and *marinara* - tomato, garlic and oregano. In America, marinara sauce is typically tomatoes, garlic and basil, but when talking about mussels in Italy, it's garlic, onions, white wine, and parsley.

Once, maritime traditions used to embrace easy, flavourful cooking, and it seems they have left their mark on modern-day Italian cuisine in this well-loved dish which takes less than 15 minutes to cook.

If you can't source fresh mussels, frozen ones are a good option, but seek out those with shells as their briny flavour really shines in the sauce (which is almost the best part). Don't forget to find yourself a big napkin, a big bowl for the shells, and a big glass of Pinot Grigio - *buon appetito!*

SECONDI

COZZE ALLA MARINARA
MUSSELS MARINARA

PREPARATION TIME: 10 MINUTES, PLUS 30 MINUTES FOR THE MUSSELS TO SOAK | COOKING TIME: 15 MINUTES
SERVES 2

INGREDIENTS

400g mussels
5 tbsp extra-virgin olive oil
1 onion, diced
2 cloves of garlic, diced
200ml dry white wine or Prosecco
2 tbsp flat-leaf parsley, chopped
Cracked black pepper, to taste

OPTIONAL
10 cherry tomatoes, halved
Crusty bread

PREPARATION

1. Scrub the mussels clean of any dirt and pull off the beards. Soak in a bowl of cold, salted water for 30 minutes to release any grit, then strain off the water.

2. Heat 2 tablespoons of olive oil in a large saucepan and sauté the onions and garlic. When the garlic begins to brown, add the wine.

3. Cook off the alcohol for a minute before putting the mussels into the pan and covering with a lid.

4. Cook on a medium heat for 3 to 4 minutes, stirring every now and then until the shells open. Add the parsley and adjust the seasoning with pepper to taste.

5. Discard any shells that have not opened and spoon the mussels and sauce into two deep bowls. Drizzle with olive oil and keep a few slices of crusty bread nearby to mop up the beautiful juices.

COOK'S NOTES

Add cherry tomatoes to turn this dish into the rosso version; you can add these in step 2 before the wine.

Menaggio, Lago di Como

POLENTA CON GORGONZOLA
POLENTA WITH GORGONZOLA

In a vast world of gorgeous cheeses, gorgonzola stands out as Italy's most classic blue cheese. *Gorgonzola dolce* is sweet, creamy, and streaked with blue-green veins of flavour. *Dolce* translates as 'sweet' but also 'soft' in Italian, perfectly describing this cheese's oozy nature. *Gorgonzola piccante* (sometimes named mountain gorgonzola) is aged longer and has a sharp, lingering flavour with an intense tang and denser consistency. It holds its shape well, especially when served beside sliced Italian meats on a *tagliere* (see page 17). The blend of sharp and sweet is quite divine when gorgonzola's striking blue marbling is coupled with figs, grapes, and honey.

To pair gorgonzola's intense flavour with humble, creamy polenta is a clever, comforting match. The tradition of mixing local melting cheeses into polenta is an ancient one which is embraced in regional recipes throughout northern Italy. In Valtellina, Lombardy, *polenta taragna* gets its name from the wooden *tarél* used to prepare their special blend of buckwheat and maize flour, melted butter, and local *casera* cheese.

Lake Como, situated nearby, is known as *Larius* in Latin and *Lario* in Italian, but few refer to it as this, except when talking 'food'. Larian cuisine features polenta as a staple and its use varies according to households and occasions, but there's one unique polenta and cheese dish you won't find on a menu – only at a party.

This rich Larian recipe and its quirky ritual incorporates so much of what's to love about Italian food culture - simple ingredients made special. The ancient tradition of '*il Tóc*' began centuries ago in the charming lake town of Bellagio, but it was only performed on special occasions such as weddings and baptisms. Farmers would come together, bringing their produce and simple wares as their contribution to the culinary event.

To start the festivities, the official *Tóc-maestro* would take their place beside a cauldron in the centre of the room and begin the very precise process. *Tóc* features the most basic ingredients cooked with the utmost skill; one slight slip of the hand and all goes belly-up.

Polenta flour and water are combined over a medium flame in an enormous pot, around which the party guests sit in a circle, as is tradition to this day. The polenta is cooked until it comes away from the sides; after which, we know it is ready, and enormous quantities of cheese and butter are stirred through with a *rodech* in a very precise manner. Making sure the butter is correctly incorporated is the crucial moment, because if not done correctly, the polenta will suddenly release the butter and become completely inedible!

Everyone is given a wooden spoon to scoop up the abundantly rich polenta. Traditionally, the party would eat it with their hands before the same maestro began *ragell* preparations in the same cauldron. Copious amounts of red wine would be poured into the pot with the addition of spices like nutmeg, cinnamon and cloves. The addition of sugar, lemon zest and an apple brings about the magical part: as the wine heats, the alcohol catches flame and the cauldron produces an extravagant, blazing show of light which extinguishes when the *ragell* is announced, '*Pronto!*' – 'Ready!'

The beverage is served from the centre of the room in a wooden bowl passed around the circle. With a celebratory sip, each guest feels united in one dish, one bowl, in one important celebration, which these days might even be Sunday lunch. Magical indeed.

POLENTA CON GORGONZOLA
POLENTA WITH GORGONZOLA

PREPARATION TIME: 10 MINUTES | COOKING TIME: 5 MINUTES FOR INSTANT POLENTA; 1 HOUR FOR TRADITIONAL POLENTA | SERVES 4-5

INGREDIENTS

375g instant polenta (for traditional, see notes)

1.6L water (approx.)

Coarse salt, to taste

50g butter, plus an extra knob

200g gorgonzola dolce or piccante

40g Grana Padano

Cracked black pepper, to taste

OPTIONAL
Thyme leaves

PREPARATION

1. Every polenta is different, and the packet should indicate how much water you need to cook it correctly. Use this as a guide to heat the required amount of water in a heavy-bottomed saucepan until boiling. Salt the water to taste and pour the instant polenta flour in a steady stream, a pioggia, whisking continuously to avoid lumps. Keep mixing until the polenta thickens – it's here you'll need to switch to a wooden spoon.

2. Cook on a medium heat according to the packet instructions, giving a good stir every now and then. When ready, adjust the seasoning and stir in a knob of butter.

3. Adjust the consistency by mixing in more boiling water and stirring to create a thick but soft polenta, though bear in mind that it will solidify somewhat on the plate. Stir half of the gorgonzola through the polenta then spoon it onto four or five plates.

4. Break or cut up the remaining gorgonzola and scatter over the top. Shave the Grana Padano atop each portion and finish with a sprinkling of thyme leaves and some fresh black pepper.

COOK'S NOTES

To make traditional polenta, a copper polenta pot is best if you have one.

Follow steps 1-2 and don't worry if a crust forms on the edges of the polenta; this is normal – just keep an eye on it. Word on the street is, when the polenta is done, this crust will pull away from the sides of the pot.

Taste test after your recommended cooking time, adjust the seasoning, and stir in a knob of butter, continuing from step 3.

MELANZANE ALLA PARMIGIANA
AUBERGINE PARMIGIANA

This is an iconic dish which many believe pays homage to the north Italian city of Parma, origin of Parmigiano Reggiano. The '*parmigiana*' in '*alla parmigiana*' refers to the cheese, not the city, as this recipe is classically 'southern'.

The age-old love story of Italian tomatoes, garlic, basil and mozzarella comes together here, layered between golden aubergines you can either fry, bake or grill. There's no official recipe as such, and due to Eggplant Parmesan's popularity in America, a thousand different versions exist of this luscious, summery main course.

Part of the magic comes from the abundance of fragrant extra-virgin olive oil which, when served in Sicily or Naples, oozes out onto your plate. Aubergines are sponges which will suck up every drop, so frying them 'the Neapolitan Way' means having lots of bread on the table for mopping up their juices – as well as red wine, of course. None of us are complaining.

My theory about the tastiness of aubergines says that they must be golden for the best flavour. My preferred method for getting them golden is to oven bake them under the grill. We use less olive oil, but they still maintain that quintessential oozy, oily quality without all the frying, bringing great taste every time. That said, the most memorable of all my aubergine experiences was Roberta's home-cooked dinner at her Guest House Malù in Scala. Some of the most beautiful parts of the Amalfi Coast are not on the coast but up the hill.

After the most decadently abundant meal one could ever ask for, Roberta sighed, looking disappointed we couldn't finish it all. In Italy, to leave the table hungry is morally wrong, so deep down she was thrilled. The next day, she sent us on our travels with wrapped-up *pizza rossa* and leftover *melanzane alla parmigiana*; a bundle that kept us fed for days.

Any aubergines are good in this dish; however, the quality of the mozzarella must be spot on. In southern Italy, scamorza or provolone cheese is equally adored, especially the *piccante* one. Italian pizza mozzarella is sold in blocks instead of packets; it contains much less liquid and is perfect in this recipe. You could also drain a packet of *mozzarelle* in a sieve, allowing them to drip dry as much as possible.

The amount of tomato sauce here is also subjective; we prefer a 'drier' portion that stands up on the plate. We also bake this the day before, so the sauces distribute well and the flavours have time to improve overnight, but every family is different. This is our recipe, which we hope you enjoy making and, *soppratutto* (above all), eating.

MELANZANE ALLA PARMIGIANA
AUBERGINE PARMIGIANA

PREPARATION TIME: 15 MINUTES | COOKING TIME: 45 MINUTES | SERVES 4

INGREDIENTS

4 cloves of garlic (2 diced; 2 sliced paper thin)

5 tbsp extra-virgin olive oil

1 x 400g tin peeled Italian tomatoes or 300g tomato passata

Salt and pepper, to taste

250g mozzarella (2 mozzarelle)

1.2kg aubergines

100g Parmigiano Reggiano, grated

1 handful of basil leaves

COOK'S NOTES

It's important to drain the liquid off the mozzarella or opt for pizza mozzarella (the block kind, not the pre-grated cheese as it's too rubbery). You can substitute mozzarella for scamorza or provolone, too.

These days, most aubergines aren't bitter. Traditionally, we used to salt them to remove any bitter juices, and you can still do this, although I've never found it necessary. If you prefer to salt them, sprinkle table salt onto the sliced aubergines after step 3, then let them rest in a large bowl or colander for 30 minutes. Wash off the salt and juices before patting them dry and continuing with step 4.

Keep for 3 days in the fridge or freeze for up to 1 month.

PREPARATION

1. To make the sauce, begin by frying the diced garlic in a saucepan with 2 tablespoons of olive oil. As soon as the garlic browns, pour in the tomatoes and squash down any whole tomatoes with a spoon. Season and cook for 20 minutes on a low heat, stirring every few minutes to create a thick sauce. If using passata, either cover the saucepan with a lid while it cooks or add spoonfuls of boiling water if it begins to dry up. While the sauce is cooking, drain the mozzarelle in a sieve.

2. Wash the aubergines, remove the tops, and slice them lengthways into 1cm-thick slices.

3. Turn the grill to a high heat. On a wide baking tray, drizzle 2 tablespoons of olive oil and arrange the slices side by side. Drizzle 1 tablespoon of olive oil over the aubergines, season with salt and pepper, and place under the grill. You can also use a grill pan here; grill each side for 10 minutes until golden, working in batches.

4. Preheat the oven to 180°c (160°c fan/gas mark 4). In a deep dish, roughly 24x24x7cm, place slices of aubergine side by side to create one layer, then spread a spoonful of tomato sauce over the top with some mozzarella, grated Parmigiano, a few basil leaves and the sliced garlic. Keep layering, making sure to keep a spoonful of tomato sauce and enough Parmigiano for the top. The layers and quantities don't need to be precise. Bake for 25 to 30 minutes until the top is golden.

5. Set aside and leave to cool slightly while the juices absorb. I prefer to bake this the day before as the flavours blend beautifully overnight. Aubergine Parmigiana is traditionally enjoyed lukewarm or even cold with bread to mop up the sauce. When reheating, turn the oven to 180°c (160°c fan/gas mark 4), cover with a sheet of foil to prevent the top from burning, and warm through for 25 minutes.

Serravalle, Veneto

CREMA DI FAVE CON CICORIA
FAVA BEAN SOUP WITH CHICORY

The bitter, leafy vegetables of the chicory family excel in their diversity of colour and shapes. As one of Italy's much-loved *ortaggi* (kitchen garden plants), you can find these to seed, grow and harvest almost all year round.

In Puglia, the heel of Italy's boot, the chicory plant is loved in a local dish named *fave e cicioria*. Here, chicory grows tall, spiky leaves and looks like an immense dandelion – indeed, the two are sisters in the same happy family. Up north, around the walled city of Treviso near Venice, the plant is tricked out of her winter lethargy in dark water tanks, forcing the tendrils to thicken and sweeten and develop into the enchantingly curvy, purple and white *radicchio di Treviso*.

Chicory plants range from bitter Belgian endive buds to frilly *endivia* salad leaves (called frisée) to *escarole*, which you can chop up and fry in garlic for a delicious bitter topping to a soup. Radicchio comes in greens, reds and whites, in variegated fronds, frills and roses. I just love the diversity of the chicory sisters – each and every one of them.

This recipe can be chopped and changed to suit you and the season you're in. In England, butter beans make a beautiful *crema*; in America, navy or great northern beans work just the same magic. Dried cannellini, haricot and broad beans can all be soaked and cooked into a smooth, soupy purée which pairs perfectly with chicory leaves in this Puglian recipe, *puntarelle* around Rome, or *catalogna* in Nonna Lili's kitchen garden.

The sweetness of the bean purée meets the bold, garlicky bitterness of the sautéed leaves, and if you love chilli, a few flakes really tops things off. Find delicious extra-virgin olive to drizzle abundantly, some bread to serve alongside, and enjoy this wholesome, vegan soup as a *primo* or *secondo* to warm the coldest of nights.

CREMA DI FAVE CON CICORIA
FAVA BEAN SOUP WITH CHICORY

PREPARATION TIME: 10 MINUTES, PLUS 12 HOURS SOAKING TIME FOR DRIED BEANS | COOKING TIME: 1 HOUR FOR DRIED BEANS; 30 MINUTES FOR TINNED BEANS | SERVES 4

INGREDIENTS

300g dried fava beans (or 500g tinned butter beans)

1-1.5L vegetable broth

5 tbsp extra-virgin olive oil, plus extra to serve

1 onion, finely chopped

1 celery stilk, finely chopped

Salt and black pepper, to taste

200g chicory leaves

2 cloves of garlic, finely chopped

OPTIONAL
Chilli flakes, to taste

COOK'S NOTES

Chicory can be substituted with cavolo nero, endive, escarole or dandelion leaves. I've also roasted fennel bulb, Belgian endive and radicchio - all equally delicious.

If you can find hulled fava beans, these only take 4 hours to soak, and you can use a fork to create a purée, as they do in Puglia. Otherwise, use a blender for dried cannellini, butter or broad beans. Dried beans are more wholesome but tinned beans are quicker.

I always make large batches of this bean purée to freeze in portions for an easy winter meal, adding whichever leafy veggies I have around.

PREPARATION

1. Soak the dried beans for 12 hours or overnight in enough cold water to double their volume.

2. After soaking, discard the water, rinse the beans well, then place them in a large saucepan. Cook in enough broth to cover them, then simmer for roughly an hour until they are soft and/or begin to break up, adding more broth if the liquid cooks away. Once cooked, remove from the heat and strain the broth into a bowl for later. Return the beans to the saucepan and set aside.

3. Fry the onion and celery in 2 tablespoons of olive oil. When the onion is soft and translucent, add the vegetables to the pot of beans. If using tinned beans, combine the vegetables and the strained beans in a saucepan.

4. Add a few ladles of the broth to the saucepan (off the heat) along with a tablespoon of olive oil and blend to a smooth purée with a handheld blender (or fork, if soft enough). Add more ladles of broth until the consistency is thick and soupy. Season with salt and pepper to taste, return to a low simmer, and cover with a lid while you prepare the chicory.

5. To cook the chicory, wash the leaves well and discard any hard stalks or wilted leaves. Chop roughly and boil in a large pot of salted water for a few minutes. Drain the leaves in a colander, then briefly run them under a cold tap to cool. Squeeze out the excess water with your hands and set aside.

6. In a pan, sauté two cloves of garlic in 2 tablespoons of olive oil (add the chilli here too, if using). When the garlic sizzles, add the cooked chicory leaves and a pinch of salt, and stir them in the garlicky oil for 1 minute.

7. Ladle the puréed beans into bowls, place the garlicky chicory on top, and serve with black pepper and a drizzle of olive oil.

CONTORNI

INVOLTINI DI RADICCHIO E PANCETTA
RADICCHIO WRAPPED IN PANCETTA

With its slender, curvy leaves, *radicchio di Treviso* is a thing of beauty and holds a prestigious place in north Italy's winter culinary bounty.

During harder times, people would naturally drift to the hills and fields to supplement their larder. As dishes and recipes developed throughout the years, foraged plants became key ingredients in traditional regional diets. In rural parts of Italy, it's typically the grandmothers who head out at sunrise. With wicker baskets, they quietly and calmly walk the pastures and pathsides looking for *funghi* on the forest floor or picking edible shoots in the spring fields. There are many *erbette spontanee* (spontaneous herbs) that are harvested according to the seasons, and the elderly know the patches they grow in, returning to them time and time again.

Plants, flowers, and mushrooms are taken home to be carefully cleaned and cooked, often ending up bottled or frozen for later use. This thrifty approach to storing seasonal food is what some say drove *radicchio di Treviso* to initially be stored in dark barns. No one is sure of how the process originated, but it's now a protected IGP product of strict production regulation within the specified provinces of Treviso, Padova and Venice.

Radicchio seeds are sown in late July and its spindly green plants are harvested in late November after the first frost, allowing time for the cross-pollination of its pretty powder-blue flowers. *Radicchio di Treviso* has always grown beside the clear, spring-fed waters of the Sile River, which are vital to further production and its geographically protected status.

After harvesting, the bushy plants are trimmed of their outer leaves, cleaned, and packed into crates or nets. They're then delicately placed into dark tanks so their roots can dangle in flowing spring water at a temperature of 15°c for 15 to 20 days. This process is known as *imbianchamento* - whitening or bleaching. The radicchio plants are 'tricked' out of their winter lethargy, but the darkness deters the growth of any green leaves, thus forcing the characteristic white flesh to thicken and sweeten, becoming crunchy. The plants are stripped of their old green foliage and trimmed down to the dark red hearts we know and adore. They are then ready for sale as the 'Flower of Treviso'.

Radicchio, of the chicory family, is known for its bitterness and can be overpowering if not paired well. Once cooked, *radicchio di Treviso* loses some sweetness and butteriness, but it gains a soft, palatable texture and a more defined bitter edge, which is perfectly matched with pancetta or salty speck as a winter *antipasto or contorni*.

INVOLTINI DI RADICCHIO E PANCETTA
RADICCHIO WRAPPED IN PANCETTA

PREPARATION TIME: 10 MINUTES | COOKING TIME: 20 MINUTES | SERVES 4

INGREDIENTS

1 head of radicchio di Treviso
4 slices of pancetta
Drizzle of extra-virgin olive oil
Salt and pepper, to taste

PREPARATION

1. Preheat the oven to 200°c (180°c fan/gas mark 6).
2. Wash the radicchio and cut the base of the stem into quarters, then gently break the leaves upwards to create four even-sized bunches.
3. Wrap a slice of pancetta around each bunch and place onto a baking tray.
4. Drizzle with olive oil and season with salt and pepper.
5. Bake for 15 to 20 minutes, or place under a hot grill. Keep an eye on the colour of the pancetta, and when it becomes golden, remove it from the heat and serve.

COOK'S NOTES

If you can't find Italian pancetta, unsmoked streaky bacon is a good substitute.

These can be made in advance and reheated quickly in a hot oven for 5 minutes just before serving.

Another option is to barbecue the radicchio on an open fire until the pancetta is cooked through.

Radicchio di Treviso can be tricky to find outside of Italy, but chicory or sliced fennel bulb are equally delicious in this recipe.

Agriturismo Claudia Augusta Altinate, Valmareno, Veneto

Val Pusteria, Sud Tirolo

INSALATA DI CAPPUCCIO CON CUMINO E SPECK

CABBAGE SALAD WITH CUMIN AND SPECK

You'll always find a big bowl of this salad in northern Italy, where the influence of German and Austrian cooking is brought to the table in dishes like Canederli (see page 123) and Spätzle (see page 131). I love to slice purple cabbage into this dish, but the traditional version is kept simple with the bold flavours of cumin and speck perfectly balancing the tang of vinegar. You can leave out the speck, as a vegetarian version is often made in South Tyrol, but to leave out the cumin would change it completely. As a Tyrolean speciality, one rather quirky trick is to use your hands in the preparation of this simple salad.

The Dolomites, where this dish is often found, are also called the 'Pale Mountains', *Monti Palidi*, but when the sun dips low and hits bare rock face, they suddenly light up to become the 'Pink Mountains'. With orangey-pink hues, dusk and dawn are spectacular around here, and the food is too. A drive through the area means enjoying produce that's local to the lush valleys and pastures, and we always look out for freshly foraged porcini sold along the roadsides, or stalls of apple sellers in autumn, their bags filled to the brim with bright Trentino apples.

I think one of the area's best combinations of tradition and food culture is the celebration of the *Desmontegada*. Roughly translating to 'come down from the mountains', the phrase refers to livestock being welcomed home in a merry parade through town after months of summer grazing. You'll see *malgari* dressed in authentic attire with their cows and horses proudly decorated in colourful wreaths and flowers. Children will sit atop hay bales piled onto wooden carts while their grandfathers play the accordion. Mothers will carry babies dressed in traditional Tyrolean bonnets, and youths will expertly steer hefty cattle and herds of goats through streets lined three-people deep. In the mountainous province of Trentino, the *Desmontegada* starts at the beginning of September, with a succession of autumnal events organised throughout the region, and each town featuring its own celebration. Hikes, shows, talks and tasting tours are planned, and then it's time to sit down and eat.

After marching through town to accordion music, clanging cowbells, and stomping hooves, everyone joins the procession towards an enormous white marquee where the animals are put to graze in designated fields. Their masters, along with the rest of us, congregate at long tables in anticipation of the glorious Tyrolean cooking about to be enjoyed for lunch.

Music, food and merriment are on the menu and, of course, this wonderful *cappuccio* salad always makes an appearance.

INSALATA DI CAPPUCCIO CON CUMINO E SPECK

CABBAGE SALAD WITH CUMIN AND SPECK

PREPARATION TIME: 10 MINUTES, PLUS 3 HOURS TO REST (IDEALLY 1 DAY)
COOKING TIME: 10 MINUTES | SERVES 4-6

INGREDIENTS

1 sweetheart cabbage

½ tsp cumin seeds

4 tbsp extra-virgin olive oil

Salt and pepper, to taste

60g speck

3 tbsp white wine or apple cider vinegar

PREPARATION

1. Peel off the outer damaged leaves of the cabbage then slice it finely with a sharp knife or mandoline.

2. Place the sliced cabbage into a bowl with the cumin seeds, olive oil, salt, and pepper, and stir to coat. Squeeze the cabbage in your hands to soften it, then put it to one side and cover with a clean cloth.

3. Finely slice the speck into ribbons, about 2cm long. If you have pre-sliced speck, even better! The finer the ribbons, the crispier they become once fried. Make sure to leave the fat on the meat, as this is what gives this salad its unique flavour.

4. Heat a frying pan and fry the speck ribbons without any oil until they are crispy and the fat has rendered. Add the vinegar, then pour all the contents onto the cabbage salad and mix well.

5. Cover the bowl and leave the salad to rest for at least 3 hours in the fridge or, if you can, overnight. This ensures the flavours combine beautifully. Before serving, check the seasoning and adjust accordingly. Store for up to 2 days in the fridge.

COOK'S NOTES

The trick to a soft, well-blended salad is squeezing the cabbage with your hands as well as leaving it to rest.

You can easily leave out the speck for a vegetarian version. Substituting it with a different cured meat isn't suitable as this regional recipe really calls for the smoky flavours of speck. If you're not using speck, add another tablespoon of olive oil and add the vinegar directly to the bowl.

CARCIOFI ALLA NONNA LILI
NONNI LILI'S ARTICHOKES

One of the most iconic of Nonna Lili dishes, after her lasagna (see page 55), is braised artichokes. Just like lasagne, artichokes always feel like a celebration. Nonna Lili likes to buy the hearts separately and cook them the same way she cooks the whole artichoke – with a special herb and garlic mix. They sell the hearts (which have been cleaned of the leaves and stem) at the market in vats of lemon water to prevent discoloration, but Nonna Lili says the lemon alters their delicate flavour, so she prefers to buy frozen artichoke hearts. This recipe uses the whole artichoke.

As the young bud of a thistle plant, artichokes nurse a baby flower in the form of a beardy 'choke' inside their fleshy leaves, but this is spiny and inedible so must be removed. Don't be put off by the mass of purple and green spikiness at the market stall; our recipe is beautifully straightforward. Once you know how to *curare* (prepare) an artichoke, each one becomes a little celebration of hard leaves you can suck the flesh out of, and its creamy heart delivers an earthy flavour unlike any other vegetable.

From the ghetto in Rome comes the sensational, deep fried, and crispy *carciofo alla giudia*, but this gently braised recipe is known simply by the rest of Italy as *carciofi alla romana* - artichokes, Roman-style. We always eat them at Nonna Lili's house, so they've become a family staple for us in Veneto too.

There is a little herb that grows wild in the fields and in cracks of ancient stone walls: a furry-leafed cross between oregano and mint. With sprays of lilac summer flowers, calamint is lovingly called *mentuccia* around Rome because it makes the sweetest partner to the famous Romanesco artichoke, *mammola*. Outside of the area, you can use a few mint leaves to recreate the flavour, or just go all-out parsley, the Nonna Lili way.

CARCIOFI ALLA NONNA LILI
NONNI LILI'S ARTICHOKES

PREPARATION TIME: 30 MINUTES | COOKING TIME: 40 MINUTES | SERVES 4

INGREDIENTS

1 clove of garlic, finely chopped

1 handful flat-leaf parsley, finely chopped

4-5 mint or calamint leaves, finely chopped (optional)

10g Grana Padano, grated

10g breadcrumbs

Salt and pepper, to taste

4 artichokes (Romanesco are best)

½ lemon, juiced

4 tbsp extra-virgin olive oil

250ml water

COOK'S NOTES

Instead of discarding the stem, Nonna Lili peels it, chops it into 4cm pieces and stands the pieces between the artichokes to cook in the same pan. Her saucepan is not high-sided, so she removes the whole stem, and you too can base the stem length on your pan's height. These braised artichokes can be eaten warm or cold and make a sumptuous side dish as well as a wonderful antipasto when sliced into chucks and placed on a tagliere (see page 17).

They keep for 3 days in the fridge.

PREPARATION

1. To make the artichoke stuffing, combine the garlic, parsley, mint (if using), Grana Padano, breadcrumbs, salt, and pepper, and set aside.

2. Peel off two rounds of the hard, outer leaves at the base of the artichoke's stem until the paler leaves begin to show. Then, use a pair of kitchen scissors to snip off the top thorny part of each remaining lower leaf.

3. Use a bread knife to take the top 2cm off the tip of the artichoke and gently pry open the leaves with your fingers (it is easier to do this under running water). Find the beardy choke at the centre of the leaves (certain types of artichokes might not have one) and use a spoon to dig out any internal hairs or spikes from the inside.

4. Cut the stem down to 5cm and 'clean' it by removing the hard skin with a sharp knife. Add the lemon juice to a large bowl of water and, as you work, immerse each artichoke in the lemon water to avoid discolouration.

5. To 'stuff' the artichoke, push it onto the table, leaf-down, to force open the leaves. Then, use a teaspoon to fill the centre of the artichoke and the gaps between the leaves with the herb and garlic mixture.

6. Find a small but high-sided saucepan (with a lid) and warm 2 tablespoons of olive oil. Pack the artichokes into the pan with their stems up and begin to brown on a high heat. When the oil is sizzling, pour in the water so that the artichoke bases are half-covered in water, then put the lid on. Turn the heat down to medium and cook for 25 to 30 minutes, intermittently adding one ladle of water so that it doesn't dry up.

7. Test the stalks are tender and a sauce has formed in the pan, then carefully turn over the artichokes and spoon some of the sauce over each one, letting the flavours soak into the gaps. Cook for another 5 to 10 minutes until most of the liquid has dried up, then remove from the heat and drizzle with the remaining olive oil to serve.

Mercato di Treviso, Treviso, Veneto

MELANZANE AL FUNGHETTO
AUBERGINES, MUSHROOM-STYLE

The first time I made aubergines 'mushroom-style' was by mistake. I had chopped the aubergines, sautéed them in garlic, and was stirring in the parsley when Francesco came home and suggested pizza. Well, naturally, I dropped the lot, put a lid on the pan, and grabbed a jacket. When we came home, the aubergines were perfect.

I believe this is the trick to one of Naples' most classic vegetarian *contorni* (side dishes). Made *rossa* (with tomato) and *bianco* (without), the description of 'mushroom- style' comes from how the aubergines are sautéed with garlic, similarly to mushrooms. The juicy texture is also similar and tastes best once you've let them sit.

The beauty of a good *contorno* is how versatile it is. You can put these onto toasted ciabatta bread with shaved Pecorino and a drizzle of extra-virgin olive oil as a delicious bruschetta, or you can stir the *rossa* version into freshly cooked gnocchi with fresh basil leaves sprinkled on top.

This recipe doesn't call for salting and straining; in fact, we rarely salt aubergines because if you choose Italian aubergines in the height of summer, there's hardly any bitterness, only a lovely umami tang that makes a delightful partner to aged, hard cheeses and grilled meats like *Tagliata* (see page 149).

Try this glorious summer staple with round aubergines like the Rosa Bianca variety; they have a sweeter flesh and less seeds. If your aubergines do have seeds, remove these before frying.

Keep *Melanzane al Fughetto* in the fridge for an impromptu *pasta fredda* with chopped sun-dried tomatoes and black olives, or add to *Un Tagliere* (see page 17) of cured meats, creamy cheeses and *Pesto di Limoni* (see page 21) for summer *alfresco* bliss.

MELANZANE AL FUNGHETTO
AUBERGINES, MUSHROOM-STYLE

PREPARATION TIME: 5 MINUTES | COOKING TIME: I HOUR 20 MINUTES | SERVES 4

INGREDIENTS

3 globe or oblong aubergines

3 tbsp extra-virgin olive oil, plus extra to drizzle

2 cloves of garlic, minced

2 tbsp flat-leaf parsley, chopped, or I tsp dried parsley

250ml vegetable stock

Salt and pepper, to taste

PREPARATION

1. Chop the aubergines into 1.5cm chunks, discarding the stalks and any hard seeds.

2. In a saucepan, heat the olive oil and fry the garlic for 10 seconds.

3. Turn the heat up and immediately throw in the aubergines and parsley, stirring gently until they begin to brown.

4. Add the stock and continue to stir on a high heat until the liquid begins to cook off.

5. Turn off the heat, put a lid on, and leave the aubergines to sit for at least an hour.

6. Before serving, warm for 10 minutes in a hot frying pan without a lid on.

7. Season to taste with salt and pepper, then drizzle with extra-virgin olive oil and serve as a side.

COOK'S NOTES

It's not necessary, but if you prefer to salt the aubergines to remove any bitterness, sprinkle them with salt after chopping and put them in a colander over a bowl for an hour. Wash thoroughly to remove the bitter juice before cooking.

If serving as an antipasto on un tagliere, these are best at room temperature.

To make the rossa version, add a handful of chopped cherry tomatoes to the pan after the garlic in step 2.

These can be kept in a container in the fridge for up to 3 days. Continue from step 6 to serve warm.

VE 9328

Venezia, Veneto

FAGIOLI BORLOTTI CON CIPOLLA
BORLOTTI BEAN AND ONION SALAD

Borlotti beans are a Veneto staple. In the area around Venice, where the plains of the Pianura Padana stretch north to touch the Prealps foothills, there are flatlands with chilly winters and muggy summers, perfect for bean growing! The love of growing your own food and having the space to do it means most gardens here have a kitchen garden, or *orto*, and most *orti* have a patch reserved for borlotti beans. Their beautiful red and white freckled skins occupy a special place in the greengrocers of this area, and they are adored for their versatility, creamy texture, and nutty taste.

There's a high plain near Belluno where the 'cream of the crop' borlotti bean is cultivated: the Lamon. This bean loves the dry, windy climate and the protection of the Dolomites' lofty, pointed peaks. Having gained PDO status, it can't be grown anywhere else but here near the border of Trentino.

Beans feature in many Italian dishes and are a prized ingredient in *cucina povera* - the inexpensive but tasty cooking style you'll notice throughout our recipe book. *Cucina povera*, 'poor cuisine', was born in harder times when people were forced to become inventive to provide nutritious food at lower costs. Times of struggle bring out a resourcefulness and a sense of community in us; one that is often lost in our day-to-day routine of eating, sleeping, making meals and making a living. I noticed this when Covid shook the world in 2020. We were in England during the pandemic; a time when the shop shelves were bare of tinned foods and restrictions were placed on flour, eggs and yeast, and when the culture of bread-making became very popular.

Bread, as one of the most basic, versatile and filling foods, is strangely pleasing to make. Perhaps the nature of yeast, that bubbles and froths, is an ancient marvel we still admire, or perhaps the smell of freshly baked bread evokes a soothing, homely feeling in us. The same can be said for wholesome home cooking, where basic ingredients are made to shine, much like the humble borlotti bean. Akin to bread in its simple but satisfying nature, the unassuming borlotti bean is beautiful when crushed, drizzled with olive oil and mixed with radicchio leaves in the Veneto classic *radici e fasioi*, or when cooked as a thick soup with short ditalini pasta for *pasta e fasioi*.

This combination of beans, onion, and lots of fresh parsley is one you'll enjoy often at our table, if the beans even make it to the table! You can substitute borlotti with pinto beans, but you should always opt for dried instead of tinned beans to truly appreciate their nutty, wholesome qualities.

FAGIOLI BORLOTTI CON CIPOLLA
BORLOTTI BEAN AND ONION SALAD

PREPARATION TIME: 10 MINUTES, PLUS 6 HOURS SOAKING THE BEANS| COOKING TIME: 1 HOUR (DEPENDING ON THE TYPE OF BEAN) | SERVES 6

INGREDIENTS

400g dried borlotti beans (see notes)

2 tbsp coarse sea salt, or 1 vegetable stock cube

2 brown or white onions, sliced

30g flat-leaf parsley, chopped

6 tbsp extra-virgin olive oil

OPTIONAL

Aged balsamic vinegar or glaze

COOK'S NOTES

Any beans are lovely here - our family favourite are borlotti, but pinto work well, as do cannellini. If you can find Lamon, they are exceptional.

Spring bulb onions (cipolotti) are wonderful in this side dish; they can be sliced and mixed in raw just before serving as they have a milder flavour.

Feel free to use this recipe to get funky with a bean salad; my mom is renowned for her famous three bean one! Add chopped carrots and celery like our friend Caroline, or add rocket, goats cheese and capers for an equally delicious combination – the possibilities are endless.

This makes an excellent accompaniment to our Easter Quiche on page 119. You can also enjoy this dish warm in the autumn with some brown bread or soft polenta.

PREPARATION

1. Soak the beans for 6 hours or overnight in cold water.

2. Discard the water and fill a pot with enough fresh water to cover the beans. Add another litre or so to double the volume, then add the coarse salt (or stock cube).

3. Turn to a medium heat and bring to the boil. Once boiling, turn down to a simmer and cover loosely with a lid (I leave a little gap so the beans do not boil over).

4. Note the cooking time for the type of bean and boil accordingly; borlotti beans take around 40 minutes. Check to make sure the beans don't overcook, but do not worry if some of them split. Remove any foam that gathers on the surface.

5. When the beans are soft but still have a little crunch, turn off the heat and add the sliced onions to the pot.

6. Once cooled, discard most of the water (you can use this as a broth base for soups) and stir in the parsley. Store the beans in an airtight container in the fridge with enough liquid to cover to keep them juicy.

7. To serve, scoop the beans and onions out with a slotted spoon and dress with olive oil and parsley. Finish with balsamic vinegar or balsamic glaze, if desired.

FOCACCIA PUGLIESE
FOCACCIA FROM PUGLIA

The art of making bread is a masterful profession and one I merely dabble in; I rely on focaccia dough which is wonderfully forgiving and turns out the most beautiful, fluffy breads every time. This recipe is inspired by the traditional focaccia of Puglia, and we make it weekly for Mangia Mangia deliveries and farmers' markets. Puglia's clever use of potato in the dough brings a soft, dense texture which holds the moisture in the bread for longer.

The regional recipe from the heel of Italy's geographical 'boot' includes durum wheat flour called semolina. Often used in pizza-making, and coarser than 00 bread flour, semolina creates a crunchy crust which perfectly marries the soft potatoes in authentic *focaccia pugliese*.

Fine semolina flour isn't easily found outside of Italy, so we use a combination of bread and plain flours for the base and a tasty pairing of cherry tomatoes and black olives for the topping, just like in Puglia's capital city, Bari. You can get creative with your condiments; think of this as a thick pizza, similar to *pizza al taglio*, a favourite street food in Rome. Anchovies, sun-dried tomatoes or slices of white onion are all delicious here, as is garlic confit, sea salt and rosemary – another of our Mangia Mangia toppings.

With three proving stages to reach its spongy heights, you'd think this focaccia was complex, but instead it's very straightforward to make. There are a few tricks to the trade, and one is your baking tray. While a round pan of roughly 25-30cm is preferred in Puglia, we like to use a rectangular aluminium tray that's at least 5cm deep. This helps the bread rise uniformly, and the thinner the aluminium, the better the rise.

You'll notice there's not much kneading in this recipe, and apart from boiling and mashing potatoes, all you need is resting time for the dough to rise, and not even that much. The heat of the cooked potatoes aids the proving process, and if your kitchen is warm, that's even better for the bread.

There's no need to get all technical here; simply follow the steps in our recipe and soon you'll have the gorgeous smell of freshly baked bread wafting through your own kitchen. Slice up your soft focaccia ready to serve beside a *Insalata Caprese* (see page 45) or a bowl of *Pesto alla Genovese* (see page 25) for an Italian foodie experience that's as memorable as the washed stone *trulli* and ancient olive groves of Puglia.

FOCACCIA PUGLIESE
FOCACCIA FROM PUGLIA

PREPARATION TIME: 15 MINUTES, PLUS 1.5 HOURS PROVING | COOKING TIME: 15 MINUTES | SERVES 6-8

INGREDIENTS

140g white potatoes

1 ¼ tsp fine salt

7g fast-action dried yeast

10g white sugar

200ml lukewarm water

200g plain flour

130g strong bread flour

6-7 tbsp extra-virgin olive oil

10-15 ripe cherry tomatoes, halved

15-20 pitted black olives

¼ tsp dried oregano

¼ tsp coarse sea salt or rock salt

COOK'S NOTES

Seek out full-flavoured Mediterranean olives like taggiasca or gaeta and take your tomatoes out of the fridge an hour before making this as their flavour will improve so much.

Ripe tomatoes will provide the most wonderful juice which is key to this focaccia.

After the first two rises, if you're feeling bread-fancy, you can scrape the dough from the sides of the bowl and fold the sides over into the centre of the ball; this traps air inside to help the alveolatura - the effect of varied bubbles in baked bread – but because we're using fast-rising yeast, folding is not essential.

PREPARATION

1. Peel and slice the potatoes, then place in a saucepan and cover with cold water and a teaspoon of salt.

2. Boil for 5 to 10 minutes until the potatoes are soft and cooked, then strain off the water and use a potato ricer or masher to create a smooth purée. Set aside to cool.

3. Prepare the yeast in a large bowl, working in a section of your kitchen with no draughts so that it can easily rise. Begin by combining the yeast and sugar with 200ml of lukewarm water. Let this sit for 2 to 3 minutes; you might see bubbles begin to form as the yeast blooms.

4. When the potato has cooled enough to handle comfortably, add it and the flours to the mixing bowl along with 1 tablespoon of olive oil and a quarter of a teaspoon of fine salt. Mix into a dough with your hands or a spoon – there's no need to knead. If the dough is dry and crumbly, add a little extra warm water and mix until moist and uniform. I like to sprinkle extra warm water onto the dough just before covering it, as this creates a humid environment to help it rise. Cover with a clean, damp kitchen towel or cling film and place the bowl in a warm spot for 30 minutes.

5. After the dough has risen, scrape down the sides of the bowl and form into a ball once again. Cover and let it rise for another 30 minutes.

6. Find an aluminium baking tray around 5cm deep (a good size is 30x20cm) and generously grease with 1 to 2 tablespoons of olive oil. You can also use a round cake tin, just not a springform one as the oil will spill out. Turn the dough out into the tray and, using your fingertips, spread it out before flipping it over so both sides are evenly coated with oil. Continue poking with your fingertips until the dough is uniformly spread, then leave in a warm spot for another 30 minutes until it has risen.

7. Preheat the oven to 220°c (200°c fan/gas mark 7), and place an oven rack between the middle and the bottom of the oven.

8. Once risen, arrange the tomatoes and olives on the dough. Squeeze the pips and juice from the last few tomatoes over the bread, then finish with a sprinkling of oregano, a scattering of coarse sea salt, and a drizzle of olive oil.

9. Check the oven is to temperature before gently placing the tray onto the rack, ensuring the dough does not flatten while you move it. Bake for 10 to 15 minutes until the top is golden and the sides are just beginning to pull away from the edges of the baking tray. Drizzle with another 1 to 2 tablespoons of olive oil and leave the focaccia in the tray for 5 minutes before sliding it onto a wire rack. Let it sit for a further 15 minutes before slicing and enjoying warm.

DOLCI

FRITTELLE DI FIORI DI ACACIA
ACACIA FLOWER FRITTERS

Two beautiful trees flower during the Italian summer and they often stand beside each other: the Italian acacia and the *sambuco*, which we know as an elderberry tree (and its flowers as elderflowers). Driving past, we'd always ask our children which were which. Both flower in spectacular sprays of white blossoms which, while differing in structure and scent, may look similar from afar.

Italian schools are usually closed for summer when these magnificent trees are in full bloom, so they've become a classic summer holiday *merenda* (afternoon snack) for young children. Since many grandparents tend to look after their grandchildren in the afternoons, it's traditionally the *nonni* who send their grandchildren out to pick *fiori di acacia* (acacia flowers) to keep them busy for a while.

The children proudly return bearing armfuls of scented branches which take time to sort through and clean. They select only the best stems to make this delicious afternoon snack: Acacia Flower Fritters.

These are the easiest and most forgiving things to throw together, and they're a good way to keep the *bambini* entertained, especially when the promise of a sugary treat follows all their foraging.

Whenever we make Acacia Flower Fritters, we can never finish them all, so we've allocated two stems per person in our recipe as it's so easy to get carried away.

In England these trees are known as false acacia. The *Robinia pseudoacacia* was introduced from America 400 years ago and grows so profusely it is sometimes considered invasive. Look out for their scented flowers – you'll be surprised how easy it is to find them – and when you do, it's time to treat yourselves to something special. Be careful to only pick the flower: **false acacia bark, seeds, and leaves contain poisonous compounds called toxalbumins and must not be consumed, especially the small seed pods which can be harmful to livestock and people.**

FRITTELLE DI FIORI DI ACACIA
ACACIA FLOWER FRITTERS

PREPARATION TIME: 10 MINUTES | COOKING TIME: 20 MINUTES | SERVES 6

INGREDIENTS

12 'false' acacia flower stems
200g plain flour
Pinch of salt
Pinch of sugar
250ml sparkling water, cold
Sunflower oil, for frying
Caster sugar, to dust

PREPARATION

1. Make sure the flowers are clean and free from insects. Discard any leaves and bottom flowers so that you have a handy, long stem to hold.

2. To make the batter, mix the flour, salt, sugar, and sparkling water together, adding the water a bit at a time and mixing with a fork until the batter has no lumps and is a gloopy consistency (enough to stick to the flowers).

3. Pour enough oil, around 6cm deep, into a pan and turn to a medium heat ready to deep fry the stems. You can test the temperature by frying a small piece of batter. When it has browned, then you know the oil is hot enough.

4. Holding an acacia flower by its stem, briefly dip it into the batter until well coated. Repeat with each flower, then quickly place into the hot oil. You can deep fry a few at a time.

5. Using a slotted spoon, remove the fritters when they begin to brown and place each one on kitchen paper to drain. Dust with sugar and eat warm.

COOK'S NOTES

Some families use self-raising flour and tap water instead of plain flour and sparkling water.

Make sure you are picking the correct flowers. **False acacia bark, seeds, and leaves contain poisonous compounds called toxalbumins and must not be consumed, especially the small seed pods which can be harmful to livestock and people.**

PANDORO ALBERO DI NATALE
PANDORO CHRISTMAS TREE

Star-shaped and golden, this traditional Italian Christmas cake has its official origins in fair Verona, but long before its creation in October 1894, 'Breads of Gold' were made all over Italy.

In Venice, 1500, during the Republic of Serenissima's reign, gold leaf was used to cover the most decadent of delicacies, including a conical cake named 'Bread of Gold' - *Pan de Oro*. In Rome, 200AD, Pliny the Elder wrote about a recipe by Chef Vergilius Stephanus Senex: '*panis*' baked with the finest flour, eggs, butter, and oil. *Pane di Vienna* was founded in northern Italy as a buttery cake, like brioche, and brought over from the Habsburg Empire in Austria. In Veneto, 1200, the star-shaped Nadalin was eaten as a dense, flat, festive cake containing no butter. Then, in 1894, Mr Melegatti from Verona created *pandoro*.

The pastry chef was so proud that he patented his cake and its star-shaped tin so it could be safely stored within the records of the Ministry of Agriculture and Commerce of the Kingdom of Italy.

Melegatti's recipe has remained unchanged since 14th October 1894 and can be bought as such in an elegant vintage tin. Over the years, the Christmas cake has been chopped and changed and filled with all kinds of things. It is now made by multitudes of bakers, but Melegtatti's recipe remains one of Verona's finest.

In shops from November and beautifully boxed, *pandoro* comes encased in a large bag with a small sachet of vanilla-flavoured icing sugar. The trick is to empty the sachet into the bag, together with the cake, and shake until the entire cake is powdery white.

Pandoro can be sliced two ways: either lengthways with everyone getting the point of a star, or horizontally, forming concentric star shapes you can masterfully stack from large to small, creating a Christmas tree. Fill every layer with *mascarpone crema*, dust your tree with more icing 'snow', and dot the corners with berries just like Christmas baubles.

PANDORO ALBERO DI NATALE
PANDORO CHRISTMAS TREE

PREPARATION TIME: 15 MINUTES | SERVES 8-10

INGREDIENTS

4 eggs, room temperature

100g caster sugar

500g mascarpone, room temperature

1 pandoro di Verona

OPTIONAL

A splash of Marsala

Raspberries, redcurrants, or blueberries, to decorate

Icing sugar, to dust (from the pandoro box)

PREPARATION

1. To make the mascarpone crema, start by separating the eggs and beating the whites until stiff.

2. In a separate bowl, beat the yolks and sugar together until light and smooth.

3. Beat in the mascarpone until all the lumps are gone, then gently fold in the egg whites.

4. Stir in a splash of Marsala if you're opting for something slightly boozy.

5. Slice the pandoro horizontally into six equal-sized discs using a bread knife. Stack them from largest to smallest with a layer of mascarpone cream between each disc, turning each slightly so that the 'branches' stick out.

6. Decorate your 'branches' with raspberries, blueberries, or redcurrants, and sprinkle with sifted icing sugar 'snow' for the full effect (there should be a bag in your pandoro box).

COOK'S NOTES

This cake takes 15 minutes to put together, so it's easily made just before serving. You can prepare the crema a day in advance and keep it sealed in the fridge, although I'd advise keeping it at room temperature for an hour before assembling as the flavours will improve.

Amaretto di Saronno, Vin Santo, limoncello or Frangelico all work well in the crema, as does the addition of crushed amaretti biscuits, orange peel, or crushed pistacchi.

Any leftover crema can be served separately in a bowl with a few biscuits to dip into it, or why not make yourself a little tiramisù?

If you can find mini pandorini, they also make adorable Christmas trees. During lockdown, we decorated a tray with three mini pandorini trees and a few reindeer biscuits to make a magical winter wonderland which everybody loved. A sprinkle of icing sugar does festive wonders!

Piazza delle Erbe, Verona

Ponte Scaligero, Verona

CROSTATA DI RICOTTA
RICOTTA AND DARK CHOCOLATE CROSTATA

Where we live in Veneto, a birthday 'cake' is traditionally a fruit crostata. These are usually ordered from the local *pasticceria*, 'pastry shop', according to the number of people expected around the table, with the option of a birthday greeting like '*Tanti Auguri*' or '*Buon Compleanno*!' in swirly chocolate writing. They are often filled with a layer of *crema pasticcera* (an Italian custard cream) and decorated with sliced seasonal fruit with a fine layer of jelly glaze to preserve the fruit. Usually, whoever's picking up the birthday crostata grabs a couple of extra *pasticcini* (pastries) while they're at the *pasticceria*, just in case there's not enough food…

To know *la crostata*, you must first know *la frolla*.

Frolla, Italy's standard sweet pastry, is used as a shortcrust base for an array of treats. It is a forgiving pastry that has a general 2:1:1 ratio of flour, sugar, and butter, with enough egg to bind. Flavours like lemon zest or vanilla are often added to the crust, but all in all, it's a straightforward thing with the filling as the main feature.

Our children love a simple crostata with strawberry, raspberry, or apricot jam. Perhaps it reminds them of birthday parties or afternoon *merenda* snacks in Nonna Lili's kitchen. Francesco's favourite is a version of ricotta and dark chocolate which is traditionally made at Easter, and it's one that our Mangia Mangia customers will recognise immediately. We initially put Italy's beloved *dolce* on our menu so that Francesco could enjoy the leftovers, but there are never any left because this crostata has become such a firm favourite amongst you, too!

Always expect a slice of crostata after a meal in a farm restaurant (*agriturismo*), mountain hut (*malga*), or village feast (*sagra*) – they're often brought out as a must with *un caffè*. If you're ever in the province of Piacenza towards the end of May, look out for signs to the Sagra della Crostata in the town of Caorso. Besides being a good old food extravaganza, there'll be singing, dancing, local competitions, and producers' stalls with desserts that are out of this world.

CROSTATA DI RICOTTA
RICOTTA AND DARK CHOCOLATE CROSTATA

PREPARATION TIME: 30 MINUTES, PLUS 1 HOUR CHILLING | COOKING TIME: 25 MINUTES | SERVES 6-8

INGREDIENTS

FOR LA FROLLA - THE PASTRY
120g white sugar
120g unsalted butter, softened
¼ tsp lemon zest
280g plain flour
Pinch of salt
1 egg

FOR THE FILLING
500g ricotta
150g sugar
1 tsp vanilla extract
100g 70% dark chocolate, chopped, or chocolate chips

COOK'S NOTES

If the frolla pastry is hard to roll, opt for the lazy way (which is how I make crostata).

While the frolla is still at room temperature and pliable, roll it flat between two sheets of baking paper and cut out a circle using the base of the tin as a guide, factoring in an extra 2cm border.

Remove the top layer of baking paper and lay the pastry (on the baking paper) into the tin.

Poke with a fork, and refrigerate. Roll the remaining pastry dough between two sheets of baking paper and, likewise, put it in the fridge until you are ready to cut out shapes. The colder the pastry, the better the crunch when baked!

Use up any leftover frolla to make biscuits.

You can also try jam or Nutella to create different versions of crostata.

PREPARATION

FOR LA FROLLA
1. Beat the sugar with the butter and lemon zest.
2. Add the flour and salt, either in a food processor or by rubbing it into the butter mixture with your fingers.
3. Add the egg, plus an extra yolk if more liquid is needed, to bind the dough. It must not be too wet.
4. Shape the dough into a ball and refrigerate for at least an hour.

FOR THE FILLING
1. While the dough rests, beat the ricotta until creamy before adding the sugar and vanilla.
2. Add the chocolate, leaving out the finest bits (the chocolate must be in small chunks).
3. Let the filling stand at room temperature until the pastry has cooled in the fridge.

TO ASSEMBLE THE CROSTATA
1. Preheat the oven to 180°c (160°c fan/gas mark 4).
2. Dust a clean surface with flour and roll out the pastry so it is about half a centimeter thick. It should be wide enough to fit a 25cm diameter tin or flat, oven-proof dish.
3. Line the tin with baking paper, then lift the pastry to cover the base of the dish and trim the edges.
4. Use a fork to poke holes into the base, then pour in the filling and spread it out evenly.
5. Roll out the remaining pastry and use cutters to form a lattice or decorative shapes, then place these on top of the filling.
6. Bake for 20 to 25 minutes until the pastry is golden.
7. Let the crostata cool completely and serve with a dusting of icing sugar.

TORTA CAPRESE
CAPRESE CAKE

Just off the coast of Sorrento, the distant, rugged paradise of Capri appears over hazy seas, beckoning you closer. Home to the most alluring of temptresses, the sirens, Capri has drawn glitz, glamour and fame since the ancient Greeks constructed an acropolis there in the 8th century BCE. Emperor Tiberius adored the place so much that he built Villa Jovis, Villa of Jupiter, as a holiday home, and who can blame him? If the crystalline waters and jagged cliffs don't tempt you enough, then the balmy Mediterranean lifestyle of lounging on terracotta terraces, dining on some of Italy's most gorgeous foods, and sipping the crispest white wines most certainly will.

In Naples, you'll spot the much-loved Torta Caprese on many *dolci* menus. The cake of Capri. Don't be swayed by its simple attire: this cake is beautifully decadent just like the isle, and it's also wheat-free.

Seldom is a prized Italian product without its romantic and enthralling legend. Much like the love-struck cheesemaker who left his curds out overnight and created gorgonzola, Capri's legendary cake owes its fortuitous creation to human error.

In 1920, a well-known local pastry chef, Carmine di Fiore, somehow slipped up and left the flour out of his chocolate and almond cake. Perhaps he was distracted by the island's sparkling waters through his bakery window; or perhaps, after a long *pausa pranzo*, 'lunch break', he'd woken up flustered after dozing in the sunshine. Some Capri residents say he was under such pressure to bake for the legendary gangster Al Capone that he messed up. Nevertheless, what resulted was a dense, chocolatey cake with a crunchy crust, much like a grainy brownie. This dessert is such a delight for the senses that, traditionally, a simple dusting of icing sugar is all that's required for this gorgeous slice of Capri confectionery.

Oranges and lemons grow so happily in this mild Mediterranean climate that everyone loves them in their cooking. Torta Caprese has been known to include a squeeze of fresh orange juice or a grate of zest, but another less traditional option is a splash of Grand Marnier or rum in the batter.

Let the cake cool completely before turning it out to avoid any breakage and then, depending on the shape of your cake tin, why not serve it the Capri way: upside-down with a dusting of icing sugar - e *basta* (that'll do!).

TORTA CAPRESE
CAPRESE CAKE

PREPARATION TIME: 30 MINUTES | COOKING TIME: 20 MINUTES | SERVES 8

INGREDIENTS

185g blanched almonds, or ground almonds (almond flour)

140g caster sugar

125g dark chocolate (70% cocoa)

125g butter

3 eggs, room temperature

½ tsp vanilla extract

Pinch of salt (if using unsalted butter)

Icing sugar, to dust

OPTIONAL

A dash of Grand Marnier or rum

1 lemon, zested

1 orange, juiced

PREPARATION

1. Preheat the oven to 170°c (150°c fan/gas mark 3). Grease and line a 20cm cake tin.

2. If using blanched almonds to make the almond flour, grind them in a food processor in short bursts to prevent the oils from separating. You can add 100g of the caster sugar at this stage.

3. Melt the dark chocolate and butter together either over a bain-marie or in the microwave.

4. In a separate bowl, beat the egg whites until they form stiff peaks.

5. In another bowl, beat the egg yolks and all or the remaining caster sugar together until light and creamy.

6. Stir in the melted chocolate and vanilla extract, then sift in the almond flour.

7. Delicately fold in the egg whites until incorporated, then immediately pour the batter into the cake tin. Bake for 20 to 30 minutes, but do not overbake as the cake will settle as it cools. Test regularly with a toothpick after 20 minutes; it is ready when the toothpick comes out clean.

8. Cool completely in the cake tin before turning out onto a plate. Dust with icing sugar to serve.

COOK'S NOTES

Because this cake has no gluten to hold the air bubbles and create a sponge, it's fundamental that your egg whites are beaten until stiff and are folded in very delicately.

One trick is to first beat the egg whites and then add half the sugar while beating at a slower speed until it is incorporated – this gives the egg whites a little more structure and helps prevent them from collapsing.

The dark chocolate must be good quality and at least 70% cocoa, as this is the most important flavour of Torta Caprese.

Italian butter is not usually salted, so add a pinch of salt to balance the flavours in step 6. This is also the perfect time to add a dash of liqueur or citrus, if using.

The flavours are best the next day, if you can wait that long!

Torta Caprese lasts 4 days covered and is best served at room temperature.

Costiera Amalfitana, Campania

TIRAMISÙ TREVIGIANO
TIRAMISÙ FROM TREVISO

Our good friend, Alessandro, lives in San Vendemiano, a small village not far from Treviso where tiramisù was originally named. In Trevigiano dialect, tiramisù literally translated means 'pick me up' - *tiramesù*. We all think Alessandro is the maestro of tiramisù because he doesn't mess around with the quantity of crema. He says tiramisù should be "*la sagra della crema*" – "the celebration of cream" – which, in this case, is mascarpone. An Italian '*sagra*' is an enormously decadent village feast with music, wine and song – if you've ever experienced one, you'll know exactly what he means.

While we all agree that the charming city of Treviso is home to tiramisù, florid descriptions of late-night brothels and weary husbands needing a 'pick-me-up' before heading home leave us uneasy with this origin story. No one can deny, however, the power of coffee, cocoa, and mascarpone in a spoon.

Some speak of the local Le Beccherie Restaurant as being the first to put tiramisù on their menu in the 1970s, and in fact they do lay claim to its global fame. Around Treviso at that time, *la sbatutin* was popular with midwives as a little whipped egg and sugar 'pick-me-up' for their patients. Some say Alba Campeol, who owned the restaurant in 1955, was given this concoction for breakfast with a strong coffee by her mother-in-law, and this is said to be the inspiration for what must now be Italy's most quintessential *dolce* of all time.

Our recipe is Alessandro's one and the one all Italians know: 4 eggs to 500g mascarpone to 100g of sugar. There are variations and, yes, you can add a little Marsala or rum to the crema, but honestly, not many of us do. When your ingredients are beautiful, your dish is beautiful, and this dessert is simply divine.

TIRAMISÙ TREVIGIANO
TIRAMISÙ FROM TREVISO

PREPARATION TIME: 45 MINUTES, PLUS 1 DAY TO SET | SERVES 6

INGREDIENTS

4 eggs, room temperature

100g white sugar

500g mascarpone, room temperature

20-30 savoiardi biscuits (depending on your dish)

1 large cup Moka coffee, cooled (250ml)

Unsweetened cocoa, to dust

PREPARATION

1. To make the crema, separate the eggs and whip the whites into stiff peaks using an electric whisk.

2. In a separate bowl, beat the yolks and sugar together for a couple of minutes on a high speed until pale in colour.

3. Spoon in the mascarpone and beat briefly until all lumps are gone.

4. Gently fold in the egg whites to finish the crema, then begin assembly, starting with the savoiardi.

5. Quickly dip each savoiardi biscuit into the coffee. Either submerge for a split second or dip one side and then the other, and layer into a 20x20cm dish that is at least 7cm deep.

6. Spoon half of the crema on top of the biscuits, spread evenly, then repeat the layers.

7. Keep in the fridge overnight and dust the top with cocoa just before serving.

COOK'S NOTES

Italians use coffee made on the stove in a Moka pot because that's what they all have at home. One seven-person Moka is enough coffee for around 20 biscuits. You can use espresso instead but dilute it with a little cold water as the coffee is not usually strong in a traditional tiramisù. If you are adding Marsala or rum, stir a splash into the crema.

To ensure your crema is nice and thick, take the mascarpone out of the fridge an hour before making the tiramisù.

If you can't find savoiardi, you can use lady fingers or boudoir biscuits. These are thinner and less 'spongy' but still work well. If you run out of biscuits, no problem! Remember what Alessandro says: "the more crema, the better".

Tiramisù is best made the day before as the biscuits have time to soften and the flavours will improve overnight.

Tiramisù lasts for 3 days in the fridge or up to a month frozen. If you are freezing it, do so without the cocoa and simply dust it before serving instead. Francesco prefers to freeze his tiramisù and then defrost it in the fridge to make the crema even thicker.

Ponte San Francesco, Treviso

Loggia dei Cavalieri, Treviso

TIRAMISÙ AL LIMONCELLO

LIMONCELLO TIRAMISÙ

One sip of limoncello takes you straight to the sun-drenched coast of Sorrento. Made by soaking local lemon rinds in sugar and alcohol, limoncello is always a good post-dinner drink option. It's classed as *un digestivo* in Italy, along with the likes of Amaro Montenegro and Lucano, but who truly knows if it 'aids digestion' or not – either way, we love it in this summery tiramisù.

Contrary to what many may think, traditional Tiramisù from Treviso (see page 225) does not contain any alcohol. So, when we were selling tiramisù from our stall on Lichfield Market Square, we'd always have people asking if it did. Some were pleased with the answer and some quite disappointed – that's when we decided to add Limoncello Tiramisù to our menu as a 2022 summer special, and now it is up there with your favourites.

Limoncello is made from lemons that grow near one of the most famous of holiday destinations: the Amalfi Coast. Winding 50km along the coast from Sorrento, the Strada Statale 163 Amalfitana, or Amalfi Drive, carries visitors along the rugged coastline to enjoy postcard views beautiful enough to take your breath away. This is not a grand road nor a particularly smooth one, but more than 5 million visitors flock here every year to gaze out at some of the most jaw-dropping, celebrated views in Italy while they queue to get into Salerno and Positano. It's a delectable wait, with a sea breeze blowing gently through the car window and the striking Amalfi sunshine sparkling on the sea. All around here, on typical *terrazzamenti*, 'terraced steps', under specially designed covers, Sorrento and Amalfi lemons grow in the fairytale-esque Lemon Gardens, *Giardini di Limoni*.

The Sorrento lemon is different to the Amalfi lemon. Though only 30km away, Amalfi lemons are exposed to hot sun and warm winds from the south, so ripen with a sweeter flavour. The official limoncello lemon, *Ovale di Sorrento*, or 'Oval of Sorrento', is named such because of its elliptic shape and is strictly controlled by the Sorrento Lemon Consortium (the *Consorzio di Tutela del Limone di Sorrento IGP*) to ensure the authenticity of its geographically protected status.

Surprisingly, the entire Sorrento lemon can be eaten, even if a little sour. Dusted with a sprinkling of sugar, it's a favourite afternoon snack for the children who play on the *piazze* around here.

TIRAMISÙ AL LIMONCELLO
LIMONCELLO TIRAMISÙ

PREPARATION TIME: 45 MINUTES, PLUS 1 DAY TO SET | SERVES 6

INGREDIENTS

5 unwaxed lemons, juiced (2 zested)

100ml limoncello

4 eggs, room temperature

100g white sugar

500g mascarpone, room temperature

20-30 savoiardi biscuits (depending on your dish)

COOK'S NOTES

To ensure your crema is nice and thick, take the mascarpone out of the fridge an hour before making the tiramisù.

You can use any lemons, just make sure they are unwaxed are as natural as possible.

If you can't find savoiardi, you can use lady fingers or boudoir biscuits. These are thinner and less 'spongy' but still work well.

Tiramisù is best made the day before as the biscuits will soften and the flavours will improve overnight.

Tiramisù lasts for 3 days in the fridge or up to a month frozen.

This recipe also works beautifully served 'in coppetta' - in little cups.

PREPARATION

1. Combine the lemon juice and limoncello and set aside.

2. To make the crema, separate the eggs and whip the whites into stiff peaks using an electric whisk.

3. In a separate bowl, beat the yolks and sugar together for a couple of minutes on a high speed until pale in colour.

4. Spoon in the mascarpone and beat briefly until all lumps are gone.

5. Gently fold in the egg whites to finish the cream, then begin assembly, starting with the savoiardi.

6. Dip each biscuit into the limoncello mixture, making sure you hold it under so the whole biscuit is soaked through. Layer into a 20x20cm dish that is at least 7cm deep.

7. Spoon half of the crema on top and spread it evenly.

8. Use the remaining biscuits, dipped in the limoncello mixture, to create the next layer and cover with the rest of the crema.

9. Grate the zest of two lemons onto the top, cover, and refrigerate overnight.

Ravello, Salerno, Campania

Marina del Cantone, Massa Lubrense, Campania

TIRAMISÙ ALLE FRAGOLE
STRAWBERRY TIRAMISÙ

For Valentine's Day, we added a deliciously fruity Strawberry Tiramisù to our menu as part of a romantic Italian meal for two. Its popularity began to grow and grow, not only on our menu but also in our own home, until we were all eagerly awaiting San Valentino, mainly for strawberry season!

It's funny to think our romantic celebrations were once rooted in the lusty Roman festival of Lupercalia, dedicated to the God of Fertility, Luperco. Much to the Catholic Church's disapproval at the time, these festivities between the 13th and 15th February involved some rather raunchy, nudist behaviour in the streets. Thus, in 496, through a tactical move by Pope Gelasio, February 14th was swiftly converted to a more sombre religious celebration: Festa di San Valentino, in honour of the church's revered saint of love and marriage. But which Valentino did they mean? For there were two.

San Valentino I was a kind, romantic soul. Born as Valentinus in the tiny town of Terni, Umbria, on 14 February in 176 AD, he celebrated love and marriage and was known for protecting lovers and encouraging large families. Religious history describes him as a healer of epilepsy and defender of love stories, but his biggest claim to fame was preventing a nasty break-up by placing a single red rose between two begruntled lovers. His gentle spirit lives on as the patron saint of beautiful Terni.

San Valentino II historically lived a far more dramatic life and died as a martyr on 14th February in 274 AD. Valentinus was a Christian priest with little regard for Catholic religion. A shame really, as there was no getting past the power of the Vatican or the Roman army in ancient times. The almost disconcertingly romantic story goes that he would marry Christian couples in secret against the church's wishes and one day conspired to marry Christian Serapia to the legendary Roman Sabino (who, truthfully, was Pagan). The ceremony was organised and conducted in haste as poor Serapia was terminally ill. Tragically, the newly-weds died in each other's arms just as Valentinus sealed their unification, but even more tragically, word got to Emperor Claudius II who insisted that Valentinus immediately renounce his faith. Naturally, Valentinus refused and was captured and imprisoned. Legend states that, after attempting to convert even the emperor himself to Christianity, the priest was beheaded on 14th February.

One cannot help but admire bold Valentinus for sticking to his faith until the very end. Thanks to Pope Gelasio, who used his martyrdom 200 years after his tragic beheading to squish an unruly Pagan party, he became a befitting mascot for loved ones worldwide who celebrate in his name every February 14th. Us foodies love to celebrate with Baci Perugina and Strawberry Tiramisù.

If you aren't fond of coffee, this lovely springtime dessert is a wonderful option and always popular with younger children. I get asked every week during strawberry season if I can make an extra one. Unlike Tiramisù from Treviso (see page 225), the strawberry version has no traditional recipe and is simply a celebration of seasonal fruits — whichever you love most. Many households chop up the strawberries and scatter them into the dessert (and on top). This is our family favourite which so many of you now equally look forward to.

TIRAMISÙ ALLE FRAGOLE
STRAWBERRY TIRAMISÙ

PREPARATION TIME: 45 MINUTES, PLUS I HOUR FOR THE STRAWBERRY SAUCE TO SIT, AND I DAY TO SET
SERVES 6

INGREDIENTS

400g strawberries

½ lemon, juiced

150g white sugar

4 eggs, room temperature

500g mascarpone, room temperature

20-30 savoiardi biscuits (depending on your dish)

COOK'S NOTES

You can use any soft fruit to make this using the same method. Other berries are also beautiful, but leave out the lemon juice if you are not using strawberries and adjust the sugar to taste.

To ensure your crema is nice and thick, take the mascarpone out of the fridge an hour before making the tiramisù.

If you can't find savoiardi, you can use lady fingers or boudoir biscuits. These are thinner and less 'spongy' but still work well.

Tiramisù is best made the day before as the biscuits will soften and the flavours will improve overnight.

Tiramisù lasts for 3 days in the fridge or up to a month frozen.

This recipe works well served 'in coppetta' - in little cups.

PREPARATION

1. Prepare the strawberry sauce by washing and chopping the strawberries. Cover with lemon juice and 50g of sugar and refrigerate for at least an hour.

2. After an hour (or more), blend the strawberries into a sauce with a handheld immersion blender. Set aside.

3. To make the crema, separate the eggs and whip the whites into stiff peaks using an electric whisk.

4. In a separate bowl, beat the yolks and remaining sugar together for a couple of minutes on a high speed until pale in colour.

5. Spoon in the mascarpone and beat briefly until all lumps are gone.

6. Gently fold in the egg whites to finish the crema, then begin assembly, starting with the savoiardi.

7. Dip each savoiardi biscuit into the strawberry sauce and layer into a 20x20cm dish that is at least 8cm deep.

8. Spoon some of the sauce onto the biscuits, spread it out evenly, then add half of the crema on top.

9. Repeat to create another layer of biscuits and crema, then cover and keep in the fridge overnight.

10. The next morning, pour the leftover strawberry sauce on top and return to the fridge until ready to serve; this keeps the colour vibrant.

Ponte Scaligero, Verona

TIRAMISÙ CON AMARETTI
AMARETTI TIRAMISÙ

As the legend goes, Giuseppe and Osolina, from the small village of Saronno, owned a baker's shop in 1719. The star-struck couple planned a commemorative biscuit to celebrate the Grand Cardinal's visit from nearby Milan, but could only find apricot kernels, sugar and eggs... so far, this sounds a lot like the Alpine innkeeper who made *canederli* on page 123. The couple fashioned a light, airy biscuit from what was in their pantry, wrapping two together in beautiful tissue paper for his Holiness. So enamoured was he that he blessed the happy couple, and they married and lived happily ever after with their unchanged and very successful recipe.

Besides the legend, even earlier evidence of the amaretti biscuit has been found in Venice. In the 17th century, Francesco Moriondo, the pastry chef to the Court of Savoy, purportedly baked an amaretto during the late Renaissance period. Whether his was apricot or almond, and regardless of which origin you choose, there's something timeless about this simple biscuit and its complex past.

Amaro means bitter in Italian. Amaretti can be made with almonds or almond paste, and they have a distinctive almondy bitterness that's balanced with their sweetness. *Amaretti di Saronno* are double baked at high temperatures – some say this is to kill the cyanide in the kernels, although no mention of this can be found in their recipes. They're dry and crumble easily, and the fact that they hold their shape until dissolving on your tongue is exactly why they're added to desserts like tiramisù. Small, simple and rounded, *amaretti di Saronno* are popular throughout the country, both within dishes and simply left out as a *biscotto di credenza* (sideboard biscuit) for any peckish passersby.

Since amaretti biscuits have always been made by the Lazzaroni family of Saronno, only they have the right to produce them under the name '*amaretti di Saronno*', amaretti from Saronno. Many versions exist across Italy: from the town of Sassello in Liguria and Piemonte comes a macaroon-style biscuit also named amaretto made with apricot kernels, egg white, sugar and almonds; from Gallarate in Lombardy (near Saronno and Milan) comes a soft version, too.

Then, there are smaller *amarettini*, some made with almonds and others using chocolate and liqueur; in fact, there's an amaretti liqueur too, and where is it from? Saronno, as in *Amaretto di Saronno*. Note '*Amaretto*', not '*Amaretti*', but one biscuit is surely one '*Amaretto di Saronno*'? The drink is now named Di Saronno to avoid confusion, but nevertheless, the Italians seem unphased by any of this malarkey because one is clearly a drink, and one is clearly a biscuit.

When I ask Francesco, "What comes to mind when we say *amaretto*?"

He says, "*Biscotto*."

TIRAMISÙ CON AMARETTI
AMARETTI TIRAMISÙ

PREPARATION TIME: 45 MINUTES, PLUS 1 DAY TO SET | SERVES 6

INGREDIENTS

4 eggs, room temperature

100g white sugar

500g mascarpone, room temperature

200g amaretti biscuits

125ml Moka coffee, cold, or 1 espresso shot, diluted with 100ml water

COOK'S NOTES

To ensure your crema is nice and thick, take the mascarpone out of the fridge an hour before making the tiramisù.

Don't be tempted to use soft amaretti biscuits as they don't hold the coffee as well.

If adding Di Saronno liqueur, simply stir a splash into the crema before layering.

I use a sheet of kitchen paper between the coffee dish and the tiramisù dish to drain off any excess coffee from the biscuit. This isn't necessary, but I prefer no coffee drips between each biscuit, especially on top.

Tiramisù is best made the day before as the biscuits soften and the flavours will improve overnight.

Tiramisù lasts for 3 days in the fridge or up to a month frozen.

This recipe also works beautifully served 'in coppetta' - in little cups.

PREPARATION

1. To make the crema, separate the eggs and whip the whites into stiff peaks using an electric whisk.

2. In a separate bowl, beat the yolks and sugar together for a couple of minutes on a high speed until pale in colour.

3. Spoon in the mascarpone and beat briefly until all the lumps are gone.

4. Gently fold in the egg whites to finish the crema, then begin assembly, starting with the amaretti biscuits.

5. Prepare a dish that's 20x20cm and at least 6cm deep. Dip the amaretti biscuits in the cold coffee to create a layer on the base of the dish, ensuring some amaretti are kept for decorating later.

6. Spoon all the crema on top and spread it out evenly.

7. Dip the remaining amaretti biscuits in the coffee and decorate the top of the dessert. Keep covered in the fridge overnight to set.

Limone sul Garda, Lago di Garda

SALAME AL CIOCCOLATO
CHOCOLATE SALAME

Something must be said for the childhood favourites where, as adults, we take a bite and are instantly transported back to lunch in Nana's kitchen or a family Christmas dinner. We find fondness in home-cooked, comfort food where the 'comfort' is mostly reminiscence.

In faded photographs of bygone birthday parties, tables are ladened with bowl of treats between bright-orange crisps and fizzy drinks, but it's the homemade bakes that always stand out; those we'd always count on to make an appearance; those that have imprinted on our memories.

Flicking through a pile of Nonna Lili's yellowing 70s prints, the focus – besides the smiling, rosy faces – is on one thing: food. Italy's beloved crostata, whether filled with apricot jam or Nutella, is a sweet staple that's guaranteed to make the party table, but another favourite that regularly takes centre stage is *Salame al Cioccolato*. And who doesn't love a good fridge cake?

Nobody really knows where *Salame al Cioccolato* originates from, which is unusual for Italy. The majority say Sicily in the early 1900s, so they've gone ahead and claimed the recipe, adding it to an ever-growing list of *Prodotti Agroalimentari Tradizionali Italiani* (Traditional Italian Agricultural Foods) by the *Ministero delle Politiche Agricole, Alimentari e Forestali* (the Minister of Agriculture, Foods and Forestry Policies). Ask any Sicilian and they'll swear it's always been theirs.

Chocolate Salame is known in Sicily as *Salame Turco*, Turkish Salame, not from its origins (allegedly) but from its dark colour. As an island stopover in the Mediterranean Sea and a link between the East, West and Africa, Sicily has always been an ancient melting pot of diversity. Before being known as Turkish Salame, it was named *Salame Vichingo*, Viking Salame, but no one quite knows why.

Many regional versions exist throughout the country, including one from Piemonte made with local hazelnuts or *gianduja*, wrapped in a net, and fondly called *'il Salame del Papa'*: The Pope's Salame. Chocolate Salame is very popular in Naples and made with rum – the recipe even features in the definitive recipe book of Neapolitan dishes, *Piatti Partenopei*. In Sicily, candied fruits are added, as are local almonds, *pistacchi*, and Marsala liqueur as opposed to rum.

We love to wrap our Chocolate Salami in festive string at Christmas, just like 'proper' salami. They're always a popular treat and make the best quirky gift for a foodie. Bring dessert on a wooden board and surprise everyone at the dinner table with this gorgeously moreish Italian classic.

SALAME AL CIOCCOLATO
CHOCOLATE SALAME

PREPARATION TIME: 20 MINUTES, PLUS 1 HOUR TO COOL AND AT LEAST 4 HOURS TO CHILL
COOKING TIME: 10 MINUTES | SERVES 6

INGREDIENTS

1 egg

50g sugar

50g milk chocolate

50g dark chocolate (70% cocoa)

10g butter

100g vanilla biscuits (see notes)

1 tsp vanilla extract

Pinch of salt

1 orange, juiced

Icing sugar, to dust

PREPARATION

1. Beat the egg and sugar together until light and creamy.

2. Melt the chocolate and butter together in a bain-marie or microwave and add the egg mixture. Mix well for one minute before removing from the heat. Leave to cool for about an hour.

3. Meanwhile, crush the biscuits (whilst still in their packet) into small chunks with a rolling pin.

4. Add the biscuits, vanilla extract, salt, and orange juice to the chocolate mixture and stir gently to combine.

5. Scoop the mixture onto a baking sheet, then roll the mixture into a salame shape and twist the ends to seal.

6. Chill in the fridge for 4 hours or overnight.

7. Unwrap the salame and dust with icing sugar. Roll in another sheet of baking paper and tie with string.

COOK'S NOTES

You can use liqueur instead of orange juice. Marsala, Frangelico, and rum all work well.

Italians traditionally use Oro Saiwa biscuits, but any plain vanilla biscuit is great. We tend to use malted milk biscuits in England.

Chocolate Salame lasts one week in the fridge and can be frozen, too.

Feel free to add chopped nuts and dried fruit like raisins, if you like.

Teatro Malibran, Venezia

FRITOLE ALLA VENEZIANA
VENETIAN CARNIVAL DOUGHNUTS

Carnival is a time rather than a day.

With excitement building from the beginning of every new year, February is known as Carnival Month in Italy, and in Venice there are two main contenders for Carnival treats: *frittelle* and *crostoli*.

Both deep-fried but very different in taste, you'll spot these Carnival favourites throughout the region in supermarkets, patisseries and bakeries as soon as the Christmas decorations come down on the Epiphany, January 4th. We may enjoy a casual *frittella* here and there in January, but when Carnival Month rolls around, we're indulging in our favourites with regular gusto until it all ends on Shrove Tuesday in a flourish of confetti, masks, costumes, and street parades.

From the Italian for fried, '*fritto*', these palm-sized dumplings are essentially a type of doughnut. Back in the 17th century, every quarter of Venice had its own *fritelero* selling freshly fried *frittelle di Carnevale* to passersby from their street pop-ups. The *fritoleri* held immense status in the city, and their coveted family recipes were exclusively handed down to their children, along with their businesses, so the tradition could continue.

The first *frittelle di Carnevale* were made with dried fruit to add flavour and were finished with icing sugar. They can still be found in Venice and are often called *fritole*, but other parts of Italy call them *zeppole* and make them according to regional preferences. In Naples, for example, they're made for Father's Day with custard crema and called *frittole di San Giuseppe*. In the island city of Venice, there's only one true type and that's the classic *fritola Veneziana*, made with raisins, pine nuts, orange peel, and the local *digestivo*, grappa. These Carnival treats are lovingly made at home by *le mamme e le nonne*, 'the mothers and the grandmothers', as soon as Carnival Month comes around.

In Venice's oldest pastry shop, Dal Nono Colussi, *fritole* are still made *col buso*, 'with a hole', just as they were in the 1600s when they were sold on a stick by the *frioleri*. You'll find *fritole Veneziane* all over the city during Carnival, with some patisseries refusing to make anything else out of pure tradition and principle.

FRITOLE ALLA VENEZIANA
VENETIAN CARNIVAL DOUGHNUTS

PREPARATION TIME: 30 MINUTES, PLUS 2 HOURS PROVING | COOKING TIME: 20 MINUTES | SERVES 10

INGREDIENTS

80g raisins

125ml grappa

230ml lukewarm milk

80g sugar

4g active dried yeast

300g plain flour

30g pine nuts

1 orange, zested

Pinch of salt

2 eggs, room temperature

Sunflower oil, for frying

Caster sugar, to dust

COOK'S NOTES

Some recipes call for candied orange peel and lemon zest. Use whichever you prefer, as they're equally Venetian.

The amount of pine nuts, raisins and grappa is merely a guide, so adjust to taste.

Feel free to use rum if you don't have grappa. You could also make fritole without any alcohol and use rum flavouring.

Twenty minutes gives the raisins a good soaking, but I find an overnight soaking to be even better.

PREPARATION

1. Soak the raisins in the grappa for 20 minutes.

2. To make the dough, start by combining the lukewarm milk, sugar and yeast in a large mixing bowl and letting it bloom.

3. When bubbles form, add the flour, pine nuts, orange zest, and salt, and beat the eggs directly into the mixture so that it is mixed well.

4. Add the raisins and grappa to the batter and cover with cling film or a damp cloth. Leave the bowl in a warm spot for up to 2 hours.

5. Once doubled in size, warm the sunflower oil in whichever pan you are using, making sure the oil reaches 4cm deep. Test if the oil is hot enough with a small blob of dough – the oil is ready when the blob turns golden.

6. Use two teaspoons to form a walnut-sized amount of dough and plop it into the oil, being careful not to burn yourself. Don't worry if the shape is not right as it will puff up.

7. Keep cooking the fritole in batches, flipping them over and removing them with a slotted spoon when golden-brown in colour. They fry within minutes!

8. Drain the excess oil by placing the fritole on kitchen paper, then dust them with caster sugar. Tuck in while still warm.

Canale Grande, Venezia, Veneto

BACI DI DAMA
LADY'S KISSES

The origins of *Baci di Dama* are rooted in Piemonte legend and date back to 1852. When King Vittorio Emanuele II tired of his usual sumptuous selection, he requested something new from the Savoy palace kitchens. His pastry chefs got to baking with what they could find, coming up with two hazelnut biscuits bound in a chocolate kiss - *Baci di Dama*, 'Lady's Kisses'.

We'll never know if these sated the King's sweet cravings, but we do know that *Baci di Dama* were first fashioned in a bakery by Augusto Manelli, not a Turin palace, and they were made with hazelnuts.

Celebrated throughout the land as a symbol of the territory, it was only natural that a dispute began as to where the biscuits specifically originated from. You see, they're famous in Italy as a regional classic from the town of Tortona, but some say Manelli first made them in Novi Ligure, 20 kilometres away, before moving to Tortona, and it was there that 'Pastry Chef Extraordinaires' Vercesi and Zanotti switched the hazelnuts for almonds. Pasticceria Vercesi named them Baci Dorati, 'Golden Kisses', and went on to win the gold patisserie award at the Milan International Trade Fair of 1906. As tradition states, they're still sold in beautiful tins from Vercesi under the old porticoes of Tortona.

Other versions of the *baci* biscuit exist, including baker Pasquale Balzola's. In 1919, Balzola created *Baci di Alassio*, 'Kisses from Alassio' – yet another town, this one on the Ligurian coast. His recipe, with egg yolks, honey and cocoa, proved so popular that he had it patented to avoid any confusion, and they're still made to the original recipe. His son Rinaldo followed in the family's footsteps and went on to bake his dad's *baci* biscuits while the personal pastry chef to the King of Italy, Vittorio Emanuele III, from 1932 to 1938. I love it when a legend goes full circle.

Baci di Dama are delicate and crumbly but hold their shape in a kiss. The ingredients are simple, but the flavour is everything in this classic, buttery biscuit with its added layer of chocolate. You can imagine the King with a bowl of these as a pick-me-up for when his regal duties weighed too heavily.

Italy is famous for so many delicacies, but there's something sweet, simple, yet perfectly balanced about Piemonte's *Baci di Dama*. Dipped into coffee or pulled apart, these cuties are wonderful to make at home and make the perfect gift.

BACI DI DAMA
LADY'S KISSES

PREPARATION TIME: 20 MINUTES, PLUS 2 HOURS CHILLING AND 30 MINUTES COOLING TIME
COOKING TIME: 25 MINUTES | MAKES 16

INGREDIENTS

75g blanched hazelnuts or ground hazelnuts

75g sugar

75g plain flour

75g butter

60g dark chocolate (70% cocoa)

PREPARATION

1. If you are grinding the hazelnuts yourself, preheat the oven to 180°c (160°c fan/gas mark 4). Toast the hazelnuts on a baking tray for a couple of minutes, checking and turning until lightly golden, then blitz in a food processor until fine crumbs.

2. Mix the ground hazelnuts, sugar, plain flour and butter in the food processor (or rub the butter in by hand) until a dough forms.

3. Tip the dough out onto a floured surface and roll into two sausage shapes. Wrap these in cling film and leave to rest in the fridge for an hour.

4. Divide the dough into small balls, weighing about 8g each, and place them onto a lined baking tray, leaving 3cm between each biscuit, then refrigerate for another hour.

5. Preheat the oven to 160°c (140°c fan/gas mark 3) and bake the biscuits from cold for 15 to 20 minutes until they have formed dome shapes and are dry to the touch. Once cooked, remove from the oven and wait 5 minutes to allow the biscuits to harden slightly. Then, move the biscuits and baking paper onto a wire rack to cool fully.

6. While the biscuits cool, melt the chocolate in a microwave or bain-marie so that it has time to thicken slightly as it cools down.

7. When the biscuits are completely cold, use a piping bag or small teaspoon to cover the flat end of one biscuit with chocolate and stick a second to it.

8. Carefully place the biscuits in the fridge for 15 minutes to set. Store in a sealed container for up to one week.

Porta Susa, Torino

Cortazzone, Asti, Piemonte

ABOUT THE AUTHOR

Writer, photographer, and passionate foodie Alison Ranwell is the owner of Italian food business Mangia Mangia ('Eat up, Eat up') and founder of 'The Italian Way', a food, travel and lifestyle blog. After 20 years in Italy, she returned to the UK to open Mangia Mangia, intent on sharing her mother-in-law's delicious lasagne. She now divides her time between Veneto and the cathedral city of Lichfield, hosting culinary evenings, mixing spritzes at summer festivals, and stocking a market stall with homemade tiramisù and Nonna Lili's lasagna. Outside of the kitchen, Alison can be found exploring Italian food markets or seeking out the lesser-known bàcari of Venice with Francesco and their two daughters, camera in one hand, Campari spritz in the other. Appetito is her first book.

www.alisonranwell.com